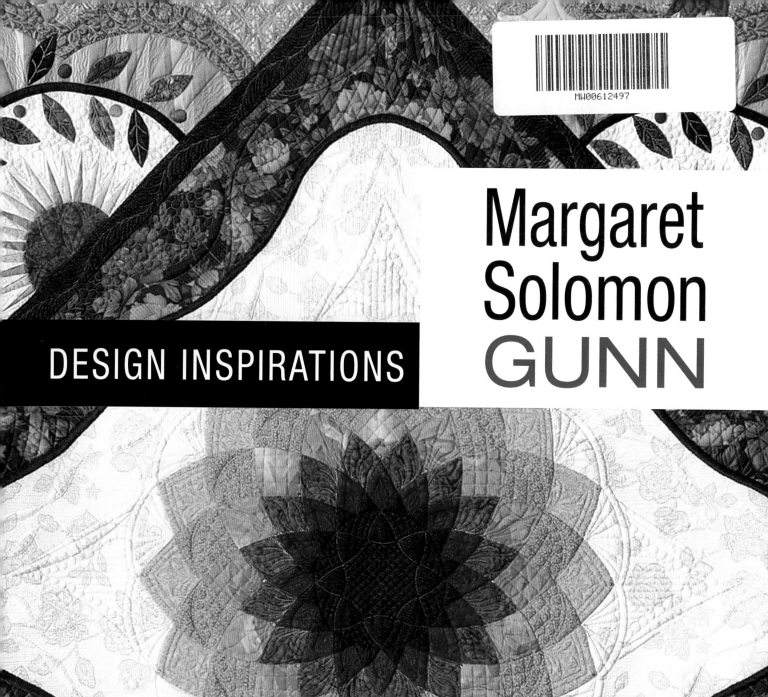

DESIGN INSPIRATIONS

Margaret Solomon GUNN

Margaret
Solomon
Gunn

A Q S Publishing

The American Quilter's Society or AQS is dedicated to quilting excellence. AQS promotes the triumphs of today's quilter, while remaining dedicated to the quilting tradition. We believe in the promotion of this art and craft through AQS Publishing and AQS QuiltWeek®.

Editor: Betsey Langford
Graphic Design: Lynda Smith
Cover Design: Michael Buckingham
Photography: Charles R. Lynch except where noted

Additional copies of this book may be ordered from the American Quilter's Society, PO Box 3290, Paducah, KY 42002-3290, or online at www.ShopAQS.com.

American Quilter's Society
www.AmericanQuilter.com

Library of Congress
Cataloging-in-Publication Data
Pending

Dedication

Many people have both knowingly and unknowingly helped me along my tremendous quilting journey, too many to name each one. A few, however, stand out with prominence.

Thanks to my family for their patience, understanding, and love. My husband barely batted an eye when I told him I wanted to spend "That Much!" on a sewing machine. He learned not to question me when I say I am going to do something. I tolerate the rantings of my teenage son who indignantly reminds me, "You're just a stay at home mom," so that I can pursue my passion while being home for my three delightful muses, more than most working moms. My fondest hope is that each of them finds a devotion for something in their lives that is half as deep as mine is for quilting.

Lastly, thanks to my mom for teaching me to sew when I was a girl, and for convincing me that if I wanted it, I could make it. She fostered my competitive spirit as a youngster, always encouraging me to try my hardest and do my best regardless if it was gymnastics, music, science fairs, or sewing. I grew up instinctively reaching for the stars, no matter how high they seemed to be. She taught me to fear nothing. She is THE Best. My mom was undergoing treatment for cancer the fall I was finishing Autumn's Surrender. The quilt was named with her very personal and challenging journey in mind – surrendering to the faith of her doctors and of eventually being healthy again.

I hope this book can convince another young quilter, like Me when I started, that anything is within your reach.

Acknowledgments

The quilting and designs may be all my own, but encouragement received from several individuals certainly contributed to my confidence and ultimate success in the business.

Thanks to:

My husband, Eric, who has somehow put up with my craziness the past seven years. I'm not sure I'd jump at the chance to let my engineer spouse purchase an expensive quilting machine and start a business with the experience I began with! Believing in me is worth everything.

Handi Quilter for giving me a fantastic longarm to create with daily.

Brenda Groelz for choosing me for Handi Quilter's advertising campaigns and letting me grace the side of HQ's truck! It's been an honor to show other quilters what your machines are capable of.

Vicki Anderson of Meandering Publishing for choosing my simple ladybug quilt entitled WHIMSICALLY FUN to be in *Machine Quilting Unlimited* magazine so many years ago. I had no way of knowing that I'd be hired to write real articles for you someday!

Scott Murkin, National Quilting Association Certified Judge (NQACJ). You have the distinction of being the only judge who has critiqued each and every one of my competition quilts—17 in all. Your comments are always trusted and have no doubt shaped the way I construct quilts.

Janet-Lee Santeusanio and Mary Schilke, who own and run what I will always consider to be my home quilt show. Machine Quilters Exposition (MQX) was the first show I ever entered and the one which keeps me constantly trying to raise the bar with my quilting. I am so grateful for being asked to teach there and share my love of creating beautiful patterns with others also.

Last but not least, I extend a huge thanks to my many trusting clients who over the past seven years allowed me to quilt for them, as I honed my skills and my love for unique intricate designs. I never would have gained the experience I have without your hundreds of quilts.

Contents

Introduction

Like many quilters, I did not just grow up and take up quilting as my profession. I arrived at this occupation via a rather circuitous path. The daughter of two math teachers, I earned multiple degrees in mechanical and aeronautical engineering, and then worked in the engineering field for nearly 15 years. I was a thermal fluids specialist, performing analyses on the Space Station project for Boeing in Huntsville, Alabama. Later, I designed and helped install commercial dryers for Metso Paper in Biddeford, Maine. I often joked that I went from doing rocket science to making toilet paper! It was mostly true. While my three kids were younger, I also taught engineering classes part time at a local university. I come from high tech, but have definite roots in the more artistic end of life.

I learned to sew long before I had a license to drive. To create things with cloth is in my blood. As a young girl, my mother taught me to embroider and to sew clothes. In high school, I made many of my own outfits, even when wearing homemade was not in vogue. When most girls were trying on different styles in the stores, I was learning to put in a zipper. I learned at an early age that I could have more clothes if I made them. While I did stop making clothes for myself, my daughter has worn many heirloom smocked dresses that I have stitched.

My first quilt was made the spring before my 1988 college undergraduate graduation. It was classic 1980s peach and blue calico Granny Squares. The corners were tied with embroidery floss, and then a drop of super glue was added to each knot to keep the knots from coming loose. The quilt was impossible to lie on top of, as the knots were very scratchy. Happily, my techniques have improved tremendously. Many quilts were made over the years for each of my children, my parents, and family. The thought of anybody having a store-bought comforter was haunting.

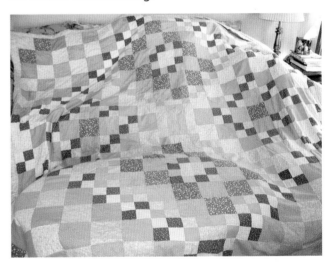

Although I have always sewn, I can't say that I was addicted to quilting until recent years. In 2007, I learned of Project Linus and quickly decided I wanted to use my scraps to make a donation quilt. My scrap box was small, so I solicited friends and family who quilted to add to my stash. By the end of 2007, I had made and donated 25 quilts. My stash, on the other hand, had grown five times its initial size! I made over 50 Project Linus quilts the following year.

While I always loved to make quilts, I cannot say the same for machine quilting. The majority of my donation quilts were tied or hand quilted, as this is what I had always done. In 2008, the purchase of a new sewing machine capable of free-motion quilting finally turned around my thoughts on machine quilting. In the next two years, I made and donated at least another 50 quilts, most of which had some amount of machine quilting. Just for fun, I had a photo shoot with the 50 plus quilts in my backyard!

During the Project Linus marathon sewing days, I also hosted a couple dozen mini quilt swaps. These swaps, coordinated through a blog on the Internet, allowed me to try my free-motion skills on smaller quilts. I was never very good on the domestic machine, but it served one purpose—to convince me I wanted something bigger. Much bigger.

While attending the summer's quilt shows, I spent time testing every longarm available, searching for the one machine that fit my criteria. I had no idea I was about to spend the cost of a car! I expected selling the idea to my husband of spending $15,000 on a sewing machine might be challenging. After all, I knew nothing about quilting with it nor about running a business.

I had been away from full-time work for the past three years and was looking ahead to the following year when my oldest son started school. I wanted a job that let me stay home with my kids, earn income, AND allowed flexible worktime while they were in school. Few corporate positions do that. Self-employment looked better and better.

My HQ Fusion® machine arrived in October 2009. One month after the longarm arrived, after quilting over a dozen practice quilts I pieced the previous summer, I officially started taking client quilts. My business, Mainely Quilts of Love, first catered to internet clients, many of whom knew me from the swaps and blog. Initially, I only took edge-to-edge quilts to gain more experience; but within a short period, I was bored with these simple quilts and began quilting feathers and other custom treatments. Simple and easy are not my nature; I need a challenge.

While my quilts stand for themselves now, seven years later, in the early days of my business many things seemed to just fall into my lap. I was approached by Machine Quilting Unlimited about featuring a quilt I made in their magazine. Photos of the quilt had been posted on a machine quilting forum. It was a simple quilt that I made for a Project Linus raffle right after I started longarm quilting. I was shocked and honored to have a quilt in a magazine; but in all honesty, I'm not sure it deserved the recognition.

I have had the pleasure of being a part of two Handi Quilter advertising campaigns, having my picture on everything from show flyers to the side of their truck! The first one, in 2010, happened largely by chance. I wrote a "My Story" essay describing how I came to have a Handi Quilter machine. The company selected 20 different people based on which machine they owned, their style of quilting, geographic location, and other demographic qualifiers. I was the

"Show Quilter." My picture was in a few magazine ads for the HQ Fusion, and the winners received a trip to Utah for a retreat. It was all very glamorous for a person that had only been longarming one year. In the winter of 2013, when my show quilts were gaining me more recognition, Handi Quilter again asked me to be a part of their advertising. Professional headshots were done, and my photo was soon gracing other advertising materials for the HQ Fusion.

Many quilters ask how and why I have come to love making quilts for show. The answers are quite simple. Four months after I started longarm quilting, I posted a photo on a quilting forum of a bed quilt I made. It caught the attention of a good quilter, who suggested I enter it at MQX, which happened to be only a few hours from where I live. In retrospect, this quilt has fairly mediocre piecing and quilting consistent with a beginner, but I was overjoyed to receive the recognition. As it turns out, this quilt, which is still on my bed, won the 2010 Rookie of the Year award. I was so surprised. More than that, I was motivated to try showing a quilt again.

Photo by Jeffrey Lomicka

Some people tell me they fear the comments that their quilt might get, so they couldn't possibly show a quilt. They believe the judging process is all about finding what is wrong with the quilt. I see this process as motivating and inspiring. My personality is different, I guess. As a former youth competitive gymnast and then adult figure skater, I am no stranger to placing my abilities under the microscope. I have performed athletically and musically much of my life. Competing quilts feels like an extension of other avenues I have taken. My next competition quilt, though, would definitely be different because it was actually designed and quilted to be a show quilt, rather than the accidental show quilt. This was the first of what would become sixteen competition quilts made since 2011!

Since 2012, Mainely Quilts of Love has been continually busy with client quilts, bringing in an increasing number of high-end custom or show quilts. I credit quilts like these for my rapidly acquired quilting skills—skills that I am able to use on my personal show quilts. Though quilting for clients is fulfilling, making quilts for shows challenges all of my creative senses. Where some quilters favor one aspect more, I love to design both the quilting and the piecing equally.

BIG BERTHA   Photo by Jeffrey Lomicka

My quilts are always original, even if they are modernized versions of traditional patterns. In 2013, I completed BIG BERTHA, a quilt featuring modernized versions of Dresden Plates. The colors are bolder, and the fabrics are large-scale modern prints. In 2015, I made BOUQUET ROYALE which is featured in this book. It is a quilt composed of elongated Hexagon blocks, made from bold large-scale fussy-cut floral prints. I enjoy working with less commonly used fabrics such as silk, hoping the uniqueness of the designs and materials will aid in setting my work apart.

BOUQUET ROYALE   Photo by Jeffrey Lomicka

Since taking up quilting, I have been published on numerous occasions. I have been a regular writer for *Machine Quilting Unlimited* magazine since late 2013, writing nearly 20 articles on a variety of machine quilting and quiltmaking topics. My show quilts have been featured in all of the industry's major quilting magazines as well.

In 2015, the process went full circle as I took my skills to the classroom and began teaching quilting. Designing and making quilts may be my true passion, but guiding others on the same quest is a very close second. I love to educate other quilters, whether in the classroom, on the quilt show floor, or on my blog.

Most days I have to pinch myself, as I still barely believe that I am living the life of a professional quilter and excelling at it happily. It has been a Cinderella story to accomplish what I have done in seven years, and I am exceedingly gracious for each person that has helped me succeed. I'm not afraid to dream big. If I can do it, you can too.

This book includes patterns for three of my more popular quilts: ZEN GARDEN, AUTUMN'S SURRENDER, and BOUQUET ROYALE. It comes almost four years after I received the first of many requests for a pattern for ZEN GARDEN. Instructions are included for making each phase of the designs using the methods I used and personally recommend. Tips are included for creating beautiful and easy appliqué as well as efficient piecing. When appropriate, patterns are included for both rotary cut piecing and paper piecing, in an attempt to appeal to the preferences of all quilters. These patterns give quilters a well-balanced variety of designs requiring both hand and machine piecing, with a range of complexity from beginner to advanced. Lastly, my original quilting motifs are provided for major sections of each quilt, and guidelines are given for all three binding techniques.

This book is about so much more than just patterns, though. It is about the inspirations for and development of the designs, as well as the techniques to execute the designs. It discusses the thought processes I used when creating the designs—both the intentional components designed initially and the ones chosen during the process when something did not work as planned. The book is about my perseverance, patience, and the importance of following one's own heart. The book showcases my journey as a quilter. To me, quilting is a passion; it is a part of my fiber and being. Quilting is a journey about color, texture, and design and all aspects share an equal importance in my finished quilts. I hope to bring readers into my world so they might better understand the thought processes I go through when creating award-winning quilts from the simple aspects of design and color, to the ornately quilted motifs I choose.

MEET ME AT GIVERNY
2012, 69" x 69"

Photo by Jeffrey Lomicka

This original, medallion star quilt was made with the bolder color palette of the Northcott Stonehenge fabrics. Purple and green are colors that are frequently seen in my quilts, as I strongly believe utilizing colors that truly speak from one's heart will always sing the loudest. The purple and green fabric used in a central border of the quilt reminded me of a Monet painting. The quilt's name is for Monet's homestead, Giverny, a place I visited on one of my trips to France. Similarly, the idea of the quilted border of sunflowers, which are abundant in France in the summer, originated from my love of France as well. The quilting deviates from my previous quilts as it is largely stitched in a contrasting gold Fil-Tec Glide thread, given to me by one of my favorite teachers, Judy Woodworth. A floral quilt motif is accented with gold acrylic paint.

BIG BERTHA
2013, 98" x 98"

Photo by Jeffrey Lomicka

This is my original design and adaptation on the traditional Dresden Plate pattern. Plates were designed to feature the fussy-cut pink centers. The quilt is made of over four dozen bold green prints pulled mostly from my stash. Approximately 90 percent of the top is hand pieced. It is quilted with nearly five miles of silk thread! This was my first of several scalloped bindings, having nearly 100 scallops and taking about 50 hours to finish. I estimate that the total quilt took me nearly 800 hours to make.

KALEIDOSCOPIC CALAMITY
2013, 38" x 38"

Photo by Jeffrey Lomicka

Made from Cross Weave fabrics by Moda I accidentally purchased and did not want to waste, this pieced quilt features many bold, solid colors. Some days its making felt like a content commingling of colors, while others it was a complete kaleidoscopic calamity! Fil-Tec Glide 40 wt. thread was used for the quilting. Much of the center of the quilt received an overlay style of quilting rather than a design that places quilting in each patch of the blocks. It is finished, as are many of my quilts, with a micro-piping at the binding.

SPRINGTIME IN THE GEISHA'S GARDEN
2014, 60" x 60"

Photo by Jeffrey Lomicka

With a curve-pieced dahlia at the center focal, a variety of taupe prints, including a stripe, damask, and another print, make up the background for floral appliqué. Appliqué is all turned edge and hand stitched. The dogwood blooms pay homage to Paducah, where a variety of soft pink fabrics were purchased to use on this quilt. While made mostly from commercial cottons, Radiance cotton/silk blend from Robert Kaufman was used as accents for the ribbon in the border, berries, and bias piping. The longarm quilting is done in several shades of silk thread, using two layers of batting to create visible texture over the many printed fabrics.

FROM THE BRIDE'S TROUSSEAU
2015, 52" x 52"

Photo by Jeffrey Lomicka

My first wholecloth, this quilt features symmetrical traditional motifs stitched on ivory Radiance cotton/silk fabric. Dozens of iterative drawings were sketched using a 45° wedge, then mirrored to create the flowing look of the many sections of this design. Green, yellow, and blue silk thread was used to bring color to the quilt through dense stitching. Some of my current quilts have dense filled Sashiko patterns in the quilting. This one has filled clamshells. Using my domestic sewing machine, a 30 wt. Superior Tire silk thread was used to quilt some details after the quilt was finished. A few hot-fix pearls finish the quilt.

THE JESTER'S FOLLY
2015, 38" x 38"

Photo by Jeffrey Lomicka

This original quilt is made from over a dozen shades of green hand-dyed Radiance cotton/silk fabric. Many pieces were small, so a scrappy approach was taken. It is a very busy little quilt, so care was taken to make the quilting and piecing cohesive. The diamond motif of the piecing was brought into the quilting in several locations. Care was also taken to soften the rigid linear piecing with plenty of curves in the quilting. The addition of small appliquéd fuchsia and blue dots creates a look reminiscent of Carnival, hence the name was born.

ODE TO SPRING
2016, 62" x 62"

Photo by Jeffrey Lomicka

Designed during the depth of a very cold and snowy New England winter, this original quilt features some of my favorite motifs of spring. Designs including flowers, dragonflies, and swirling feather sprays are symmetrically placed to interlock. The freehand quilting is stitched on lavender Radiance cotton/silk fabric using hot pink Glide thread for major motifs and three shades of silk thread for the denser fills. The dragonflies were hand painted after the quilting to increase their prominence.

THE TWISTED SISTER
2016, 80" x 80"

Photo by Jeffrey Lomicka

Made as a follow-up quilt to BOUQUET ROYALE, this quilt also features hand-stitched, fussy-cut hexagons. I did not want the hexagons to be reminiscent of a Grandmother's Flower Garden in any way. Stars were created from the hexie clusters by setting them on two unexpected fabrics, a zebra print and a green Radiance cotton/silk fabric. The stars were then appliquéd onto champagne cotton/silk Radiance with an asymmetrical twisting border. While the quilt and BOUQUET ROYALE share similarities of silks and fussy-cut hexagons, the styles are boldly different, as real life sisters can be!

Zen Garden

65" X 65"

Inspiration, Design Process, and Finishing

A little background information is necessary to understand the inspiration for making ZEN GARDEN. In 2011, my first quilt created for competition—CARTOLINE DA VENEZIA (translated as Postcards from Venice)—was attending shows and receiving critiques.

I poured my heart and every ounce of skill I had into making this quilt. Made from many of Northcott's Stonehenge collection fabrics, the quilt was my rendition of an Italian inlaid floor. I attended a couple of shows that spring and saw my quilt hanging among its competition. It was a proud moment, but one thing I took away from the shows after seeing the winning quilts was that many of them sported more color and more vibrantly contrasting colors. My quilt was muted shades of brown, terra cotta, and gray, reminiscent of concrete and stone. It seemed drab in comparison. I am a strong proponent of not making quilts specifically for what you believe the judges want to see. You must make designs you love and use colors and fabrics that spark the flame inside of you. However, browns and grays were not my colors whatsoever. I knew my next quilt would be different.

> *"I am a strong proponent of not making quilts specifically for what you believe the judges want to see. You must make designs you love and use colors and fabrics that spark the flame inside of you."*

Between 2008 and 2010, the store serving as the drop-off point for the Project Linus donation quilts gave each person ¾ yard of fabric for every quilt donated. I received about 40 yards of fabric for my last pile of donations. Many of these fabrics were bolder prints, florals, and other fabrics which I thought were pretty enough to select, but had yet to find a way to make into a quilt. These would be used in ZEN GARDEN, which would feature colors that are true to me: purples, greens, and pinks.

Construction on ZEN GARDEN began in the summer of 2011. I made myself a vow when I started this quilt to only use fabrics in my stash. This limiting decision was borne out of not wanting to spend money on fabric when I had so much piled up in my studio.

Several years earlier, I saw an episode of Alex Anderson's *Simply Quilts* where she and her guest made an easy strip-pieced Lone Star quilt. I enjoyed watching this show in the mornings while tending to my toddler and baby. I made my version of this quilt as a gift for my mother in 2006. I always wanted to make another for myself but incorporating many of the things I learned in the process to improve the placement of color.

I am not exactly sure when the design migrated from a simple Lone Star to a Carpenter's Star with 24 pieced diamonds added in the outer border. I drafted a section of the pieced diamonds using a scrapbooking program, carefully coloring the patches to match the fabrics I hoped to use.

Being able to visualize how the colors graduated through the diamonds was valuable and earned the quilt the name BLOOMING CARPENTER'S STAR. The visualization also allowed me insight on where to place pops of color, where unexpected contrast can create visual interest. I loved how the surprising simplicity of this quilt's piecing was masked beneath the mature way the colors moved.

I designed the eight setting squares to include appliqué. I wanted this quilt to be more competitive, which I felt this additional technique afforded. I also loved the way the appliqué blocks created a secondary and very dominant design. I had only been hand appliquéing a couple of years, but the techniques I learned in a 2009 Karen K. Buckley class were an invaluable stepping stone on my path to absolutely loving hand appliqué. At this time I was a busy mom, sitting many hours a week at classes or therapy for any one of my three children. Having a take-along appliqué project kept me busy.

I do not believe in making a competitive quilt that is what I think the judges want. I am not immune, though, to the knowledge that quilts with more difficult, appropriately placed, and well executed techniques tend to compete better. I know that ZEN GARDEN is a more stunning quilt on account of the appliqué squares. I also know that the degree of difficulty and use of a variety of quilting skills makes the quilt more competitive.

During the construction of the top, only one thing was a perpetual bother. It was not the two dozen Y seams as one might expect but rather the ugly tan background fabric I used. Today I would definitely purchase the background fabric that I want, but in 2011 I was holding true to my vow of not buying fabric for the top. As it turns out, the one and only fabric I had in my stash over 1½ yards was that horrible tan! Once the top was all pieced, I knew I had to do something to cover up as much of the tan as possible. I had never undertaken a huge appliqué task, but that was what it was going to take!

I drafted a serpentine vine and floral border. Smaller sections of the strip-pieced diamond sections were pieced into flowers. I used these flowers to bring additional colors into the quilt. I used nearly all the bits of fabrics from the star diamonds, and had practically nothing left of these fabrics to tie the flowers into the quilt. The last thing I wanted was to add appliqué with colors that did not coordinate. Only four of the original star fabrics were used in the flowers. Due to the scrappy nature of the quilt, this turned out to be fine.

To complete the garden appearance, butterflies were hand appliquéd near the flowers. These butterflies were fussy cut from another piece of fabric. They were the ideal size, but were not quite the color I desired. Using Sharpie® pens, I colored them to better match the quilt, heat set the fabric, and appliquéd them into place. The butterfly bodies received some embroidery to make them look dimensional, but their antennae were added during quilting. The butterflies and their respective quilting serve to break up the background and add visual interest.

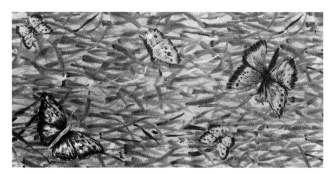

Beautiful quilting is all about finding the balance of busy and calm, of geometric and curving features, and of color. A quilt with proper balance will give the viewer's eye a reason to wander, as well as provide a place to rest. I gravitate toward symmetrical designs, especially medallion-based patterns, as these more often satisfy my sense of balance. ZEN GARDEN has a strong center focus, both in color and design. I intentionally used the same deep green for both the center of the star, appliquéd vine, and binding because the eye is instinctively drawn back to the center after it sees the outer areas of the quilt.

Looking back, I am still amazed that I quilted this quilt before I had two years of longarming experience. The designs I chose were simple, yet appeared elegant. Retrospectively, the quilting on ZEN GARDEN was relatively pain free. Typically, I remember all of the many times I had quilts off the frame to unstitch sections, and there was none of that.

I used a newly acquired Wacom® Bamboo Tablet to electronically sketch quilting ideas prior to quilting. A close up photograph was taken of an area of the quilt.

It was then opened using Photoshop® software. The tablet's pen enables electronic drawing directly onto the photograph. One design was sketched on one layer and another design on another layer. This allowed me to view the layers independently. The quilting design was sketched in a highly contrasting color so it was visible. This image should in no way imply I planned to quilt in bright yellow!

The quilting of ZEN GARDEN falls into two main areas, creating interest on the tan background and making the quilting show on the star.

One of the biggest challenges I faced with the quilting of ZEN GARDEN was how to create quilting that would show on the many printed fabrics. The quilt is double batted with Hobbs 80/20 Heirloom® batting and wool, so achieving adequate texture was not an issue. This is the standard recipe for battings which I use on all show quilts, even to this day. Texture on busy prints, however, also shows better if quilting motifs are more geometric. Parallel lines and grids show better than feathers. The line work increases prominence when every other line or space is back filled. I did this in a couple of areas on ZEN GARDEN in the appliqué setting squares and on the outer diamonds that make up the star. One thing I discovered is that quilted pebbles on prints create plenty of nondescript texture but none of it is discernable as a definite design. The three larger circles placed within the spread of smaller

pebbles should have had denser stitching around their periphery. It would have made the large circles more apparent.

I wanted ZEN GARDEN to have sections of filled curved crosshatching in the background. This stitching design is reminiscent of spider webs which seemed fitting for the quilt. The presence of the appliqué complicated the stitching of these, as there were not open spaces on the background without leaves and flowers in the way. Allowing the crosshatching to lie behind the appliqué was worth the effort and has become a signature border treatment that I frequently choose.

Being early in my quilting career, I constantly looked to other good quilters for inspiration. I do not believe copying their work is ideal, so I would study their style and then take my thoughts to my personal drawing board. Karen McTavish was very popular for her McTavishing design. My rendition of a similar fill which I was using on quilts combined a pseudo-McTavishing with sections of pebbles. This stitched up quickly and gave a light, fluttery appearance behind the butterflies. To further identify the placements of the butterflies, long parallel line contrails were quilted to help define their flight path. These served to break up the background, making the presence of the butterflies more evident.

All of the quilting on Zen Garden was stitched with WonderFil™ InvisaFil™ thread, a 100 wt. polyester. This thread is very, very fine. When stitched, it barely shows at all, leaving just the texture of the quilting behind. I love this thread for areas with very dense stitching, such as the filler placed between the radiating lines. It also created a beautiful texture on what I believed was a bland tan background, bringing this seemingly boring color to life.

"Every quilt made brings lessons of one form or another."

Learning how to effectively quilt on prints was undoubtedly Zen Garden's largest lesson for me. I discovered that I should try quilting with a heavier thread. A thread with a sheen might also add a pleasing dimension on top of the prints. There is a fine line between creating quilting with visible texture and that which overwhelms and is excessively thready. A wise quilter would make a sample diamond of the prints to test quilt prior to starting the actual quilt. Lastly, quilting on prints requires simplifying the design. Remember single lines of stitching do not show. Double lines show, but only a little. To see lines of quilting, consider multiple lines of parallel stitching. A simple rule will make texture that much more evident. Lines of stitching spaced ¼" or less will go to the negative, while lines spaced in excess of ¼" will become positive, the puffy part of quilting. The eye discerns texture when there is a clear delineation between the two. Allowing parallel lines to be greater than ¼" apart has a more pronounced effect.

More than four years after the quilting, with the lessons from quilting nearly 200 quilts, this photo shows how I might design it today for more visual quilting.

Awards

Best of Show, Quiltfest of Jacksonville, 2015

Best Wall Quilt, AQS QuiltWeek - Des Moines, 2014

Best Machine Quilting, AQS QuiltWeek - Lancaster, 2014

Best Mixed Media (Pieced & Appliqué), Vermont Quilt Festival, 2012

Best of Judged & Exceptional Merit, Maine Quilt Show, 2013

Best of Show (Images), Lowell Quilt Festival, 2013

1st Place, Quiltfest of Jacksonville, 2015

1st Place, AQS QuiltWeek - Grand Rapids, 2014

1st Place, NQA, 2014

1st Place, Georgia Quilt Show, 2013

1st Place, Minnesota Quilt Show, 2013

1st Place Color Compatibility, A Quilters Gathering, 2012

2nd Place, AQS QuiltWeek - Chattanooga, 2014

2nd Place Machine Quilting Excellence, A Quilters Gathering, 2012

2nd Place Overall Craftsmanship, A Quilters Gathering, 2012

2nd Place, Quilt Odyssey, 2012

3rd Place, Shipshewana Quilt Festival, 2015

3rd Place, AQS QuiltWeek - Charlotte, 2014

Honorable Mention, Indiana Heritage Quilt Show, 2013

Honorable Mention, AQS QuiltWeek - Paducah, 2013

Honorable Mention, MQX East, 2012

Honorable Mention, HMQS, 2012

Assembly

ZEN GARDEN is a modified Carpenter's Star. Its many different fabrics give it a scrappy appeal. Gradual color gradations are necessary to help the star bloom. The Carpenter's Star has a neutral background embellished with appliqué vines and flowers.

The Star is comprised of two basic units of construction:

Diamond Units: Eight Diamond Unit A sections make up the central star. The outer star has 16 Diamond Units B and 8 C sections. All diamond sections are strip pieced from different fabrics.

Tulip Setting Square Blocks: Eight Tulip Setting Squares attach outboard of the central star. These squares involve both piecing and appliqué.

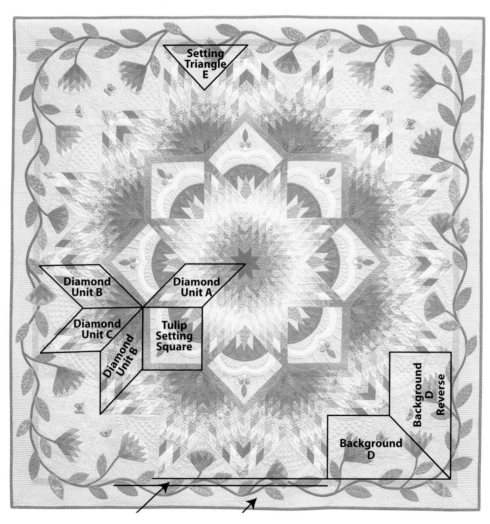

ZEN GARDEN Fabrics: (33 colors plus scraps)

10 shades of green plus 6-8 medium to dark green scraps for leaf appliqués

6 shades of pink/rose

7 shades of purple/magenta

3 shades of gold

1 pale yellow

2 shades of brown

2 shades of aqua

Tan background

Tan Print

Use the charts below to locate the specific fabrics used.

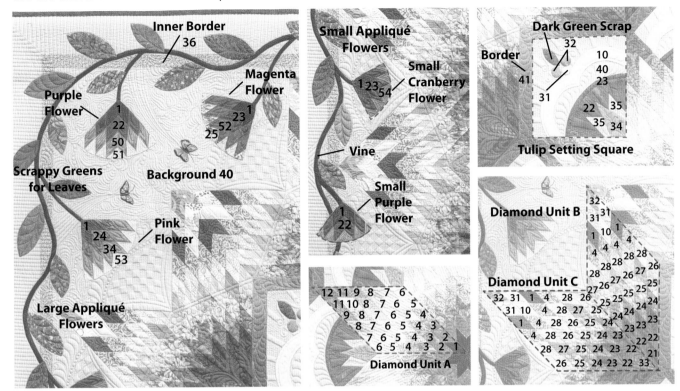

Fabric Requirements:

Color	Quantity	Location
#1 Dark green	1⅔ yds	Diamond Units A, B, C Bias vine and Appliqué border flowers 29" x 29" square for binding
#10 Pale yellow	½ yd	Scallop on Tulip Setting Squares Diamond Units A, B & C
#22 Deep purple	¾ yd	Background of Tulip Setting Square Large and small appliqué border flowers Diamond Units B & C
#23 Deep magenta	⅝ yd	Bias trim on Tulip Setting Squares Large and small appliqué border flowers Diamond Units B & C
#34 Medium pink	¼ yd	Pieced tulip on Tulip Setting Squares Large pink appliqué border flower
#35 Soft pink	⅛ yd	Pieced tulip on Tulip Setting Squares
#36 Tan print	⅜ yd	Inner border
#40 Tan	3 yds	Tulip Setting Squares, E, D & G
#41 Medium green or ombre	¼ yd	Borders on Tulip Setting Squares
Medium/dark green scraps	⅝ yd total	Appliqué leaves
Batting	70" x 70"	
Backing	Wide goods – 2¼ yds 40" yardage – 4⅓ yds	

Strip Yardage Requirements (assumes full 40" width):

Color	Yardage	Cut into 1½" x 40" Strips (Qty)
#2 Medium dark green	⅛ yd	2
#3 Medium green	¼ yd	3
#4 Green	½ yd	10
#5 Light green	¼ yd	5
#6 Pale green	⅓ yd	6
#7 Light gold	¼ yd	5
#8 Medium gold	¼ yd	4
#9 Dark gold	⅛ yd	2
#11 Brown	⅛ yd	2
#12 Dark brown	⅛ yd	1
#21 Deep bluish purple	⅛ yd	1
#24 Medium magenta	½ yd	7
#25 Rose	⅝ yd	8
#26 Sage green	¼ yd	5
#27 Slightly darker sage green	¼ yd	8
#28 Pale green	½ yd	8
#31 Light aqua	¼ yd	3
#32 Medium aqua	⅛ yd	2
#33 Medium cranberry	⅛ yd	1
#50 Purple	¼ yd	See Cutting Instructions for flower Pages 32–33
#51 Pale purple	⅛ yd	
#52 Cranberry	⅛ yd	
#53 Pale pink	⅛ yd	
#54 Deep rose	⅛ yd	

Cutting Instructions:

Cutting Chart for Tan Background Fabric #40 (3 yds)

Cut the long G pieces from the fabric first, then cut the remaining pieces.

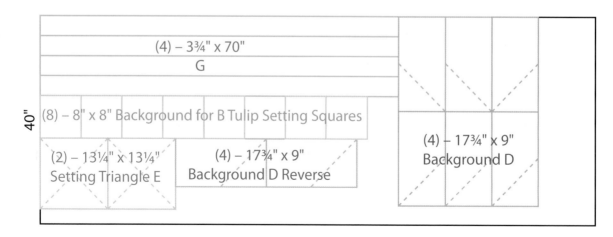

Cut the following pieces from the tan background D rectangles. Cut 4 of each.

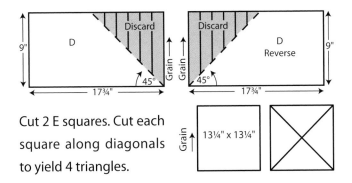

Cut 2 E squares. Cut each square along diagonals to yield 4 triangles.

Tulip Setting Square (Make 8)

Block finished size: 8½" x 8½"

Templates and patterns on pages 30–31

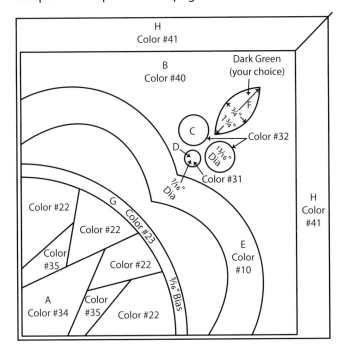

This block consists of:

A – Tulip Units 1 and 2 quarter circle

B – (1) 8" x 8" color #40 tan background square

C – (2) 1¼" diameter color #32 medium aqua circles, finishing ¹³⁄₁₆" diameter

D – (1) ⅞" diameter color #31 light aqua circles, finishing ⁷⁄₁₆" diameter

E – (1) Color #10 pale yellow scallop

F – (1) dark green leaf (use scraps from the outer border appliqué leaves)

G – (1) ¾" x 8" color #23 deep magenta bias strip, finishing ⁵⁄₁₆" wide

H – (16) 1½" x 9½" color #41 border strips, finishing 1" (Note: these strips are longer than needed. Can be trimmed after the corner is mitered.)

A – Tulip Appliqué (Make 8)

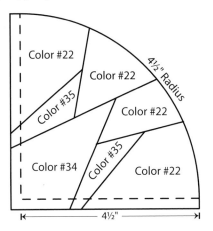

Note: The ¼" seam allowance is given for two straight sides. The seam allowance is not needed for the curve because the edge is covered with bias trim.

Paper piece Tulip Unit #1 and Tulip Unit #2. Trim each unit to size.

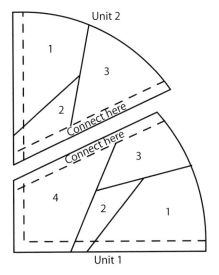

Stitch Unit #1 to Unit #2 where indicated on the pattern.

Place the Tulip appliqué on the 8" x 8" background square, aligning the unit with the edges of the square. Baste ⅛" from outer edges along the entire perimeter. Machine baste if preferred.

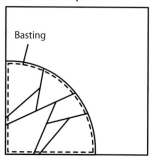

G – Bias Trim for Setting Squares

Start with a 12" square of color #23 deep magenta. Starch it twice. Then cut along the diagonal.

Reposition and stitch together. Press seams open and trim to ⅛".

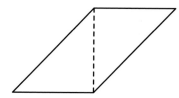

Cut (8) ¾" strips along the bias edge.

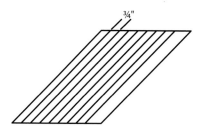

With the right sides out, gently fold both sides in on themselves, folding the strip into thirds. Do not press. This is my preferred method. The more common way to

make bias strips is to pull the strips through a 5⁄16" bias maker and press. If this is a method you are comfortable with, then feel free to use it.

Hand baste through all three layers to hold them in place. It requires a little hand gymnastics, holding the folded fabric in one hand, while basting with the other.

Don't press until after stitching the bias trim onto the block.

Place the bias trim over the tulip appliqué basting, aligning with the curve. Pin. Hand or machine stitch the inner curve first. Trim back any of the tulip background that peeks out of the top side of the bias strip. Pin and hand or machine stitch the outer part of the bias curve. Remove the basting.

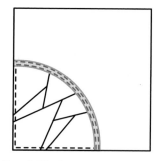

C & D – Appliqué Circles

Cut circles from color #32 medium aqua fabric in the following sizes:
16 Circle C – 1¼"
8 Circle D – ⅞"

Prepare the turned edges using the Preparing Turned Edge Circles Tutorial found on pg. 155

F – Leaf

Use the template on pg. 30 to make the template. Make a template the finished size of F. Cut the leaf from dark green fabric about 3⁄16" to ¼" bigger than the template.

Prepare the turned edges using one of the appliqué preparation techniques given in the Preparing Turned Edge Appliqué Tutorial found on pg. 155.

To applique the point of the leaf, press or glue the seam allowance for one of the seam allowances, then fold the remaining flap at the point so it is beneath the patch. DO NOT CUT the extra fabric off at the points.

E – Scallop Appliqué

Using the Scallop template on pg. 31, cut the scallop from color #10 pale yellow fabric about ³⁄₁₆" to ¼" bigger than the template.

Prepare the upper and lower turned edges using one of the appliqué preparation techniques given in the Preparing Turned Edge Appliqué Tutorial on pg. 155.

The ends of appliqué scallop go into the block seams so they do not need to be turned under. Appliqué elements should be pinned to the square and attached either with hand stitching or by a machine stitch. For hand stitching, choose a 60-100 wt. thread that matches the appliqué patch color.

Adding Borders to the Setting Square

Two sides receive 1" finished borders.

Cut (16) 1½" x 9½" rectangles from color #41 medium green fabric. These are oversized and will be trimmed after the miter is stitched.

With right sides together, place the first strip of the border as shown. Stitch to a ¼" from the right end and stop. Backstitch a couple of stitches.

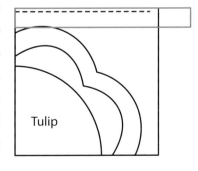

Press the seam toward the border.

Place another border strip right sides together on the square and only stitch to the point where the block meets the first border. Backstitch a couple of stitches.

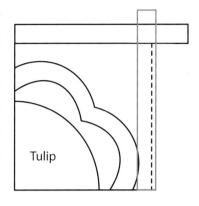

Press the seam toward the border.

Using a cutting guide with a 45° angle line, position the miter precisely and press.

Glue baste, press, and then machine stitch the angle or hand stitch the miter.

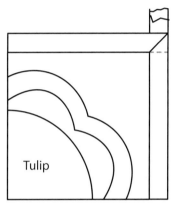

Press the seam open along the miter.

Trim the excess to ¼" along the miter.

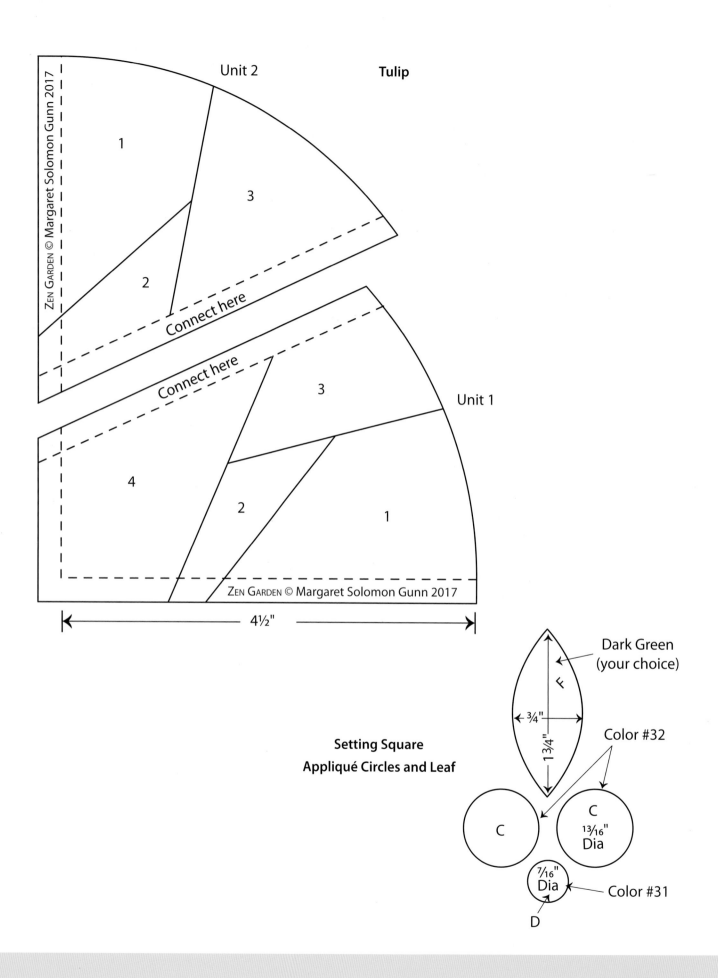

Unit 2

Tulip

1

3

2

Connect here

Connect here

3

Unit 1

4

2

1

ZEN GARDEN © Margaret Solomon Gunn 2017

ZEN GARDEN © Margaret Solomon Gunn 2017

4½"

Dark Green
(your choice)

F

¾"

1¾"

Color #32

C

C
¹³⁄₁₆"
Dia

Setting Square
Appliqué Circles and Leaf

⁷⁄₁₆"
Dia

Color #31

D

E – Scallop Appliqué Template

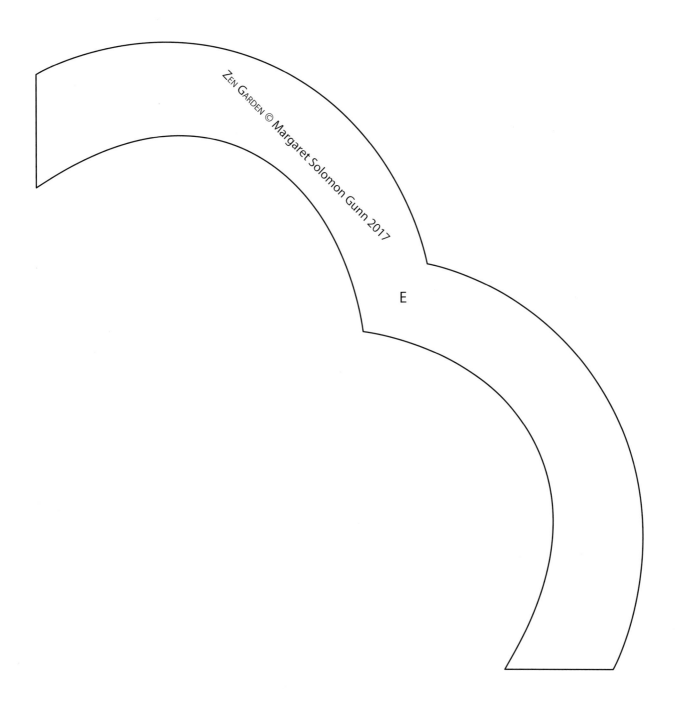

Zen Garden © Margaret Solomon Gunn 2017

E

Diamond Unit A

Cutting Instructions

Color	Cut strips 1½" x 21" (Qty)	For Strip Set
#1 Dark green	1	A-A
#2 Medium dark green	2	A-A, A-B
#3 Medium green	3	A-A, A-B, A-C
#4 Green	4	A-A, A-B, A-C, A-D
#5 Light green	5	A-A, A-B, A-C, A-D, A-E
#6 Pale green	6	A-A, A-B, A-C, A-D, A-E, A-F
#7 Light gold	5	A-B, A-C, A-D, A-E, A-F
#8 Medium gold	4	A-C, A-D, A-E, A-F
#9 Dark gold	2	A-D, A-F
#10 Pale yellow	1	A-E
#11 Brown	2	A-E, A-F
#12 Dark brown	1	A-F

Diamond A Strip Sets – All Strips are 21" long. Offset each strip about 1" when sewing together. Trim the strip set ends at a 45° angle.

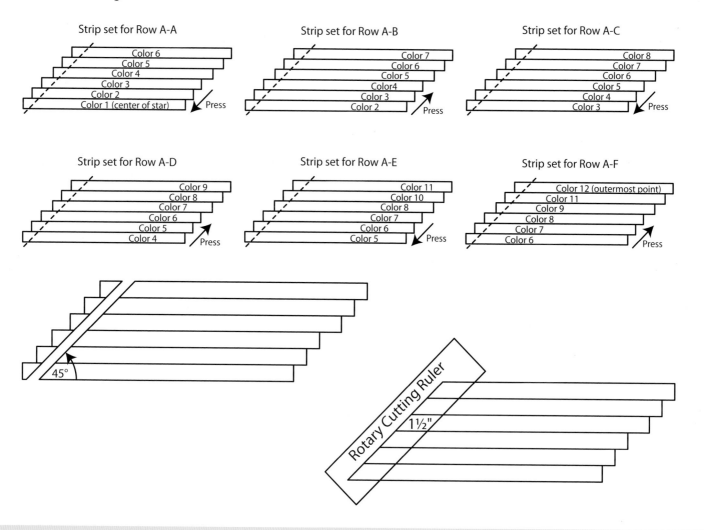

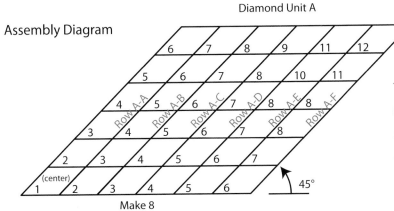

Diamond Unit A

Assembly Diagram

This unit is for the center star. Make 8 of these units. The unfinished size of this unit should be 9" along each of the four sides (8½" finished). Numbers indicate fabric colors.

Make 8

Diamond Units B & C

Cutting Instructions

Color	Cut 1½" Strips from 40" WOF	Make # of Strips Total Length Required	For Strip Set
#1 Dark green	3	2 strips 60" long	B-D, B-F
#4 Green	6	4 strips 60" long	B-C, B-D, B-E, B-F
#10 Pale yellow	2	1 strip 60" long	B-E
#21 Deep bluish purple	1	1 strip 40" long	B-A
#22 Deep purple	1	1 strip 40" long	B-A
	2	1 strip 60" long	B-B
	1	1 strip 21" long	C-A
#23 Deep magenta	1	1 strip 40" long	B-A
	3	2 strips 60" long	B-B, B-C
	1	1 strip 21" long	C-A
#24 Medium magenta	1	1 strip 40" long	B-A
	5	3 strips 60" long	B-B, B-C, B-D
	1	1 strip 21" long	C-A
#25 Rose	1	1 strip 40" long	B-A
	6	4 strips 60" long	B-B, B-C, B-D, B-E
	1	1 strip 21" long	C-A
#26 Sage green	1	1 strip 40" long	B-A
	3	2 strips 60" long	B-C, B-E
	1	1 strip 21" long	C-A
#27 Slightly darker sage green	5	3 strips 60" long	B-B, B-D, B-F
#28 Pale green	8	5 strips 60" long	B-B, B-C, B-D, B-E, B-F
#31 Light aqua	3	2 strips 60" long	B-E, B-F
#32 Medium aqua	2	1 strip 60" long	B-F
#33 Medium cranberry	1	1 strip 21" long	C-A

*For 60" strips, bias seam strips together to make 60" strips. After the 6-piece diamond strips are cut from the strip sets, if there was one with a seam, discard it. On the busier prints, many times the seams do not show.

Strip Set Diagrams

Diamond Units B/C

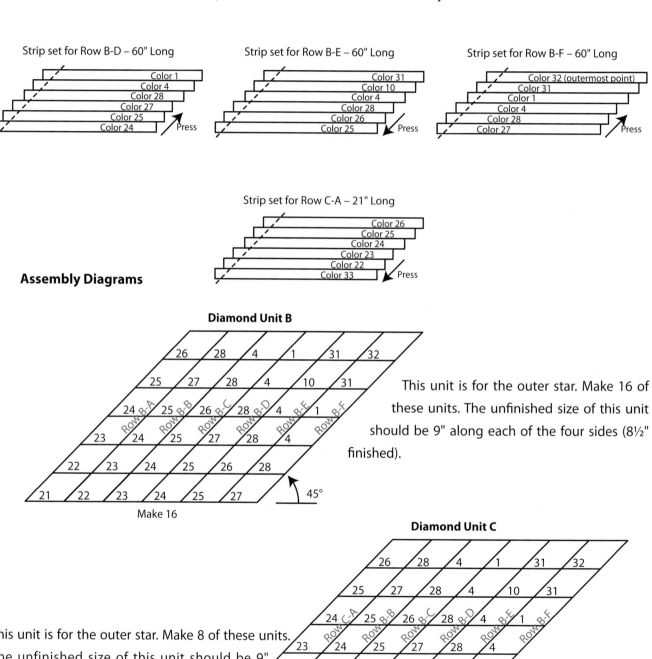

Strip set for Row B-A – 40" Long

Color 26
Color 25
Color 24
Color 23
Color 22
Color 21
Press

Strip set for Row B-B – 60" Long

Color 28
Color 27
Color 25
Color 24
Color 23
Color 22
Press

Strip set for Row B-C – 60" Long

Color 4
Color 28
Color 26
Color 25
Color 24
Color 23
Press

Strip set for Row B-D – 60" Long

Color 1
Color 4
Color 28
Color 27
Color 25
Color 24
Press

Strip set for Row B-E – 60" Long

Color 31
Color 10
Color 4
Color 28
Color 26
Color 25
Press

Strip set for Row B-F – 60" Long

Color 32 (outermost point)
Color 31
Color 1
Color 4
Color 28
Color 27
Press

Strip set for Row C-A – 21" Long

Color 26
Color 25
Color 24
Color 23
Color 22
Color 33
Press

Assembly Diagrams

Diamond Unit B

This unit is for the outer star. Make 16 of these units. The unfinished size of this unit should be 9" along each of the four sides (8½" finished).

Make 16

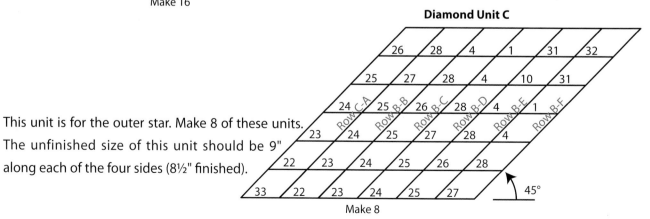

Diamond Unit C

This unit is for the outer star. Make 8 of these units. The unfinished size of this unit should be 9" along each of the four sides (8½" finished).

Make 8

Assembly of Quilt Center

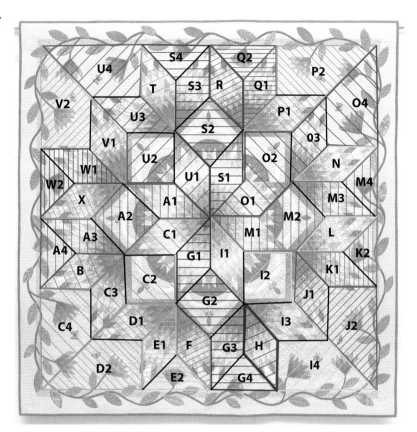

This schematic shows the order in which sections should be assembled. All appliqué of the Tulip Setting Squares and Diamond Units A, B, and C must be complete.

Each block has an assigned location shown in the chart above. Beginning with the A blocks assemble them according their number, piecing A1 to A2 then individually adding A3 and A4. This creates assembly A. Continue this process for all the blocks assembling each according to their letter to make C assembly, D assembly, E assembly, and so forth. B, F, H, L, N, R, T, and X are single blocks and not part of an assembly.

Once all the assemblies are made, attach the assemblies together in alphabetical order A through L.

Half of the top is now connected. Set this large unit aside. Follow the same directions starting with the M pieces to create a unit of remaining blocks.

You now have the entire top, minus two borders, pieced into two large sections.

Piece the two sections together.

Sewing Y Seams

Y seams are necessary when a piece must be added to another and a single straight seam will not work. ZEN GARDEN has 135° Y seams.

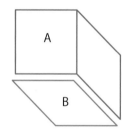

To connect B to A, place the B unit right sides together on A. Start stitching at the left edge of the fabric stopping when the needle goes exactly into the seam joining the two A sections.

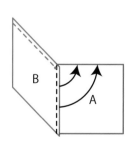

With the needle in the down position, pivot the fabrics gently easing the sides of B to the edge of A as indicated with arrows. Continue sewing the seam pinning as needed.

The Borders
Inner Border
The #36 tan tonal print fabric should be a subtle print and blend with the #40 tan background.

From the full width of the starched yardage, cut 7 strips 1½" wide.

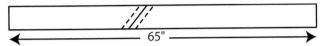

Piece these together to yield 4 strips 65" long each. Miter the joining seams and press open. This reduces bulk and makes the border lie flatter and straighter.

Border Units
Attach the inner border F and outer border (cut previously from the #40 tan background fabric) to each other. The outer border is longer.

Center the inner border on outer border as shown below.

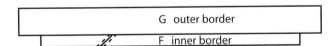

The ends will be mitered after the unit is attached to the quilt

Make 4 border units.

Adding the Borders
Add one border unit, centering on the quilt. The borders will be too long intentionally.

Sew the border unit to the quilt starting and ending ¼" from the edge of the quilt. Backstitch at each end.

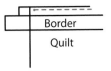

Press toward the outer borders.

Add the border opposite this one following the same instructions.

Add the third border, stitching only from where the seam meets the inner border. This makes it easier to press the seam open when mitering.

Press the seam outward.

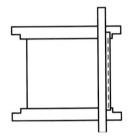

Add the last border following the same technique used for the third border.

Miter borders starting with one corner, folding the borders to the same side. Use a rotary cutting guide with a 45° line, adjust the miter until aligned and the corner is square. Press.

Glue baste this into position and heat set with an iron. From the backside, machine stitch along the crease. Trim off the excess and press the miter open.

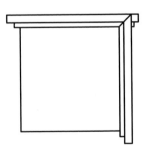

Do the same techniques for the remaining corners. The quilt is now ready for appliqué vines and flowers.

Asian Flowers & Vines Appliqué Outer Border

Large Flowers

◯
◯
◯

Small Flowers

◯
◯

Design Requires:

36 Large leaves

48 Small leaves

300" of ⅜" continuous bias for the main vine

120" of ¼" continuous bias for the vines
    to each flower

12 Large flowers

8 Small flowers

The large and small flowers are constructed in different colorways. Those are strip pieced from 1½" strips in a similar manner to the Diamond Units. Quantities of strips are given in the following tables.

Cutting Instructions for Flowers:

Cut 1½" Strips for Large Flowers

Colorway #1 makes 4 large pink flowers.

Color	Quantity	Length
#1 Dark green	1	15"
#24 Medium magenta	2	15"
#34 Medium pink	3	15"
#53 Pale Pink	4	15"

Colorway #2 makes 4 large purple flowers.

Color	Quantity	Length
#1 Dark green	1	15"
#22 Deep purple	2	15"
#50 Purple	3	15"
#51 Pale Purple	4	15"

Colorway #3 makes 4 large magenta flowers.

Color	Quantity	Length
#1 Dark green	1	15"
#23 Deep magenta	2	15"
#52 Cranberry	3	15"
#25 Rose	4	15"

Cut 1½" Strips for Small Flowers

Colorway #1 makes 4 small cranberry flowers.

Color	Quantity	Length
#1 Dark green	1	15"
#23 Deep magenta	2	15"
#54 Deep rose	3	15"

Colorway #2 makes 4 small purple flowers.

Color	Quantity	Length
#1 Dark green	1	15"
#22 Deep Purple	2	15"
#50 purple	3	15"

Large Flowers

Make 12

The large flowers are constructed from 1½" strips similar to the Diamond Units. These instructions make 4 flowers.

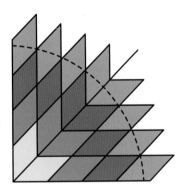

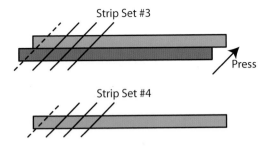

Strip Set #3

Press

Strip Set #4

ZEN GARDEN has 12 large flowers, 4 in each color combination. This yields a nice scrappy look.

For the 4 large flowers, cut (8) 1½" strips from each of the 4 strip sets shown above.

Stitch the sections with the * together first, pressing all seams one direction.

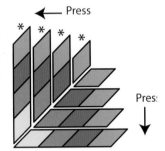

Press

Press

Stitch the next 4 sections together and press.

Sew these 2 units together pressing the seams to one side. Avoid pressing the seams open as this complicates stitching in the ditch when quilting.

Repeat the process to make 12 large flowers.

The finished flower has an approximate 5¹¹⁄₁₆" radius. You can make a template from clear pattern plastic to mark where the curved side should be turned under.

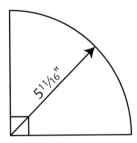

5¹¹⁄₁₆"

Hand or machine appliqué the flowers in place with all edges turned under.

Strip Set #1

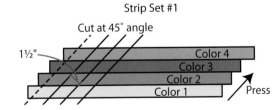

Cut at 45° angle

1½"

Color 4
Color 3
Color 2
Color 1

Press

Strip Set #2

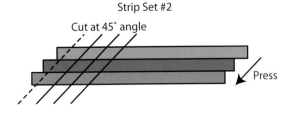

Cut at 45° angle

Press

Small Flowers

Make 8

Zen Garden has 4 small flowers of the cranberry colorway and 4 purple. These are constructed identical to the large appliqué flowers, but only three strip sets are needed.

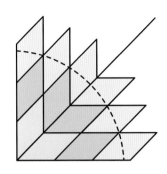

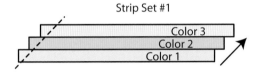
Strip Set #1
Color 3
Color 2
Color 1

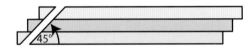
45°

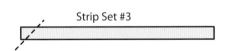
Strip Set #3

For the 4 small flowers, cut (8) 1½" strips from each of the three strip sets shown.

Strip Set #2
Press

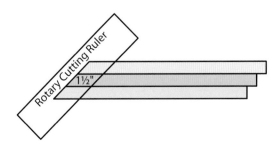
Rotary Cutting Ruler
1½"

Stitch 3 units with the * together first, pressing seams one direction.

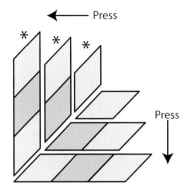
Press
Press

Stitch the other 3 pieces together.

Stitch 2 units together along the diagonal seam.

Repeat the process to make 8 small flowers.

The finished flower has a 4¼" radius.

Appliqué Leaves

The dark line on the templates is the finished size. The dashed line is the size to cut for turned edge.

The leaves on Zen Garden are turned edge. They are a scrappy mix of medium and dark greens. Some of them are from the piecing of the diamonds and some of them are from my stash.

There are many ways to appliqué the leaves. I chose to hand stitch them with turned edges. The edges were painted with starch and pressed around Templar® heat-resistant plastic.

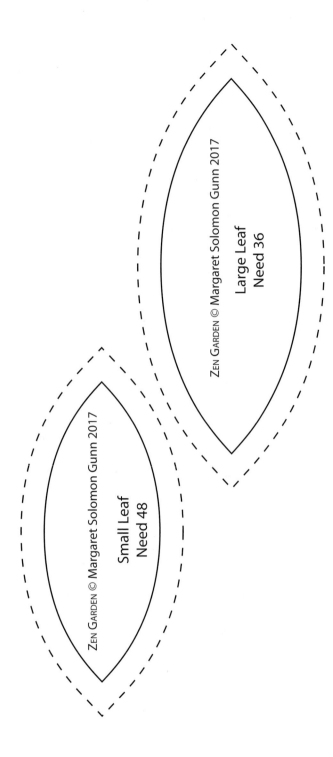

Zen Garden © Margaret Solomon Gunn 2017

Large Leaf
Need 36

Zen Garden © Margaret Solomon Gunn 2017

Small Leaf
Need 48

Bias Stem for the Outer Border

The larger bias vine is ⅜" wide, 300" of continuous length is needed.

Cut a 25" square of #1 dark green fabric.

Press and starch the square.

Cut the square in half along the diagonal.

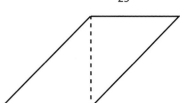

Reposition the triangles as shown and stitch them together.

Press the seams open.

Place the rotary cutting guide along the diagonal and cut (10) 1" strips. Save the remainder of the bias fabric for the ¼" bias stems.

Stitch the strips together into a continuous strip with a short stitch length. Press each seam open and trim the seam excess to about ⅛" to reduce bulk.

Using the instructions on page 28 describing how to make the bias strips for the setting squares, make the continuous strip into a turned edge bias vine.

The ¼" bias stems led from the primary serpentine ⅜" vine to the 20 flowers requiring about 120" of ¼" bias.

Use the remaining fabric from what was prepared for the ⅜" bias vine. Cut (4) ¾" strips.

Prepare the turned edge bias vine by the method of your choice.

Position the flowers, bias stems, and main vine around the border, tucking the end of the stem beneath the main vine and flowers. Attach the stems first, then the main vine using the hand or machine method of your choice. The flowers are attached last.

Quilting Motifs
ZEN GARDEN

Detailed quilting steps and illustrations are included for the Tulip Appliqué Setting Squares, the Feathered Crosshatch background, and the Outer Border components. These are the most visible areas of the quilt. Quilting on the central star and diamond units B & C is heavily masked by the printed fabrics.

Tools Required:

- Air or water erasable marking pen and/or chalk marking pencil
- ¼" straight longarm template with ¼" etched lines
- 1" diameter longarm circle template or 1" circle drawing template
- 4", 6", 8" and 12" diameter longarm circle or arc templates (12" must have etched arcs for curved crosshatching)
- Ray longarm template or protractor for marking 10° rays

Tulip Appliqué Setting Squares

There are eight Tulip Appliqué Setting Squares and each is quilted identically. Typically, the first thing I do when quilting a block like this is to outline stitch in the seam, or stitch in the ditch (SID), all appropriate features. This stabilizes the layers of the quilt, keeping them from shifting. It prepares the block for whatever detailed quilting will be done. For this block, each piece of the appliqué and each section of piecing on the tulip and border are SID, as shown by the blue lines in the illustration on the next page. Even the outline of the block itself is SID.

The SID on ZEN GARDEN is stitched using a Madeira Monolon clear nylon thread. Clear nylon is extremely fine and essentially invisible. If you accidentally stitch out of the ditch and onto a neighboring fabric patch, it does not show as much as another colored thread would. Clear polyester thread works almost as well as the nylon. I believe the nylon has a lower sheen and is slightly less visible. If you dislike working with clear threads, there are other options that can also work well for SID. These threads include 100 wt. silk, 100 wt. WonderFil InvisaFil™, or Superior's 60 wt. Botton Line, in a shade matching the ditch fabric. The ditch fabric is the one the appliqué is stitched to, OR the fabric sitting lower at the pressed seam (i.e. the seam is pressed toward the higher fabric).

Now the block is ready for decorative quilting. Mark the Swirly Detail surrounding the dark green oval, as well as the 10° rays. Size the Swirly Detail pattern so that the long side of the dark green oval is 1¾" long.

Once properly sized, mark the Swirly Detail onto the quilt top using a light box. As an alternative, a small cardstock or clear plastic template could also be created of this design. Trace the outline of the template using a marking pen.

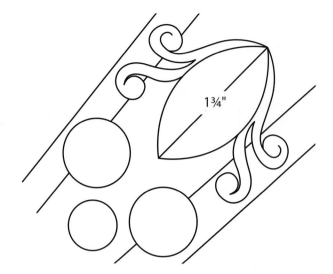

Swirly Detail Pattern

The placement of the 10° spaced rays may be marked one of two ways. Either enlarge the illustration to the exact scale of the Tulip Appliqué Setting Square, or mark the rays with a template such as Linda Mae's Ray Template. Rays on the dark purple fabric are most easily marked with chalk. I prefer the inexpensive chalk that was once used in schools, since it contains no wax and always comes off fabrics. Sharpen it to a point with an old rotary cutter. The light tan fabric can be marked with an air or water erasable pen.

The rays in each section may be continuously stitched without stopping and starting after each ray. Simply travel in the ditch of the piecing or the ditch beside the appliqué to the next ray position. Using a very fine thread such as the Wonderfil InvisaFil 100 wt. allows nearly invisible traveling in the ditch. Additionally, the threads closely match the fabric colors, purple for the lower section and tan for the outer region. Remember to stitch the Swirly Detail first, then the rays.

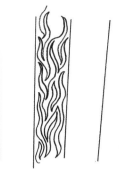

Squiggly Line Fill

Spaces indicated with "FILL" in this illustration are densely filled with the Squiggly Line Fill. This filler, which is stitched to resemble flames, consists of densely stitched wiggly and random lines, intended to push this section of the quilt to the negative space, thereby popping the neighboring ray to the positive space. This technique of alternately filling spaces increases the visibility and presence of the rays. If you prefer your quilt to have less dense quilting, this fill may be omitted and the rays will still be a beautiful background.

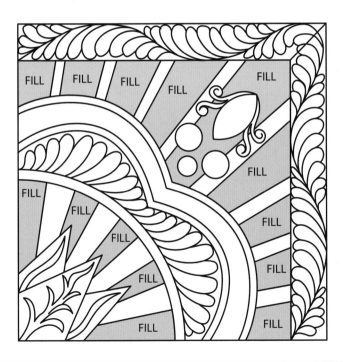

The detail stitching on the pieced tulip petals is stitched in pink thread. Note that each of these three sections can be stitched in one continuous path, beginning at the blue dot. Trace along the ditch as indicated to travel from one section to the next. I stitched this decorative detailing in a rose 50 wt. thread, but any thread of your choice would be lovely.

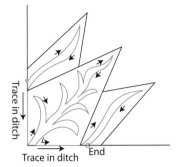

Next, quilt the feathers. Take care to ensure that the feathers located between the bias strip and the arching appliqué flow in the same direction on all eight Tulip Appliqué Setting Squares. Stitch 1-2 rows of tight echo around the ends of the feathering to help to set off the motif.

Feathers on the 1" green border can be continuously stitched for all of the eight blocks. I recommend marking the location of the serpentine spine first. While I used a wave template to mark the curve, it is flowy enough that you can eyeball the shape, giving it a natural look. Casual quilters may choose to stitch these as spineless feathers, allowing the stitching of the feathers to create the spine. For a show quilt, though, I suggest first stitching the spine and then stitching the feathers. A variegated thread in shades of green creates a lovely look for an undulating feather.

The last detail for this block is one often omitted, but I feel it adds to the finished look. Add lines of echo quilting to the appliqué arch. The lines are placed approximately 3/16" from each edge on the appliqué. Stitch these curves using the closest circle template that is of an appropriate size. This stitching creates additional texture and makes the large appliqué look less floppy.

Feathered Crosshatch Motif

Photo by Jeffrey Lomicka

There are 16 feathered crosshatch motifs on ZEN GARDEN. The motif is placed in a way that it appears to disappear behind the appliqué flowers. As a result, some marking is necessary to make the pattern appear continuous. I have made stitching as continuous as possible, tracing over existing lines of quilting when necessary rather than tying off and restarting. If the quilting is stitched using a fine coordinating 60-100 wt. thread, the retracing will be essentially unnoticeable. Bear in mind, this tutorial describes the stitching paths assuming there are no flowers obstructing the pattern; you will have to work around the appliqué, starting and stopping as necessary.

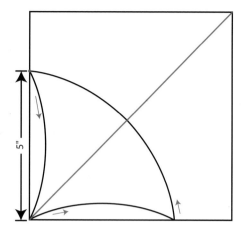

A reference line is sketched at approximately 45° as shown. This line serves as a guide while crosshatching. Most crosshatching templates have a marker etched line perpendicular to the curve that may be aligned with the reference mark.

The continuous design starts at a point indicated by the red dot, 5" from the corner. Using the 12" arc, stitch from the starting dot to the corner and out to a point 5" from the corner in the opposite direction. Place the same 12" arc between this point and the initial starting point and stitch.

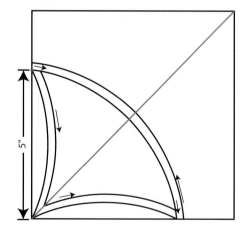

Now add a ¼" echo frame to all three arcs. Trace ¼" along the largest arc. Placing the 12" arc template at the first line of stitching, stitch an echo line following the initial two arcs. Retrace until you are at a position ¼"

outboard of the largest arc and stitch another ¼" echo.

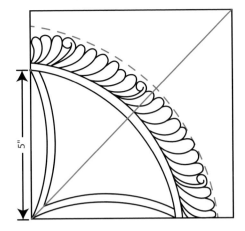

Place guide marks, shown in red, about 1" from the large outer arc. These will guide you in how tall to make the feathers. Using the outer arc as a spine, stitch feathers along this outer arc. I threw in randomly spaced hooked swirls to give the quilt a less-than-formal feeling. Feel free to quilt your favorite feather.

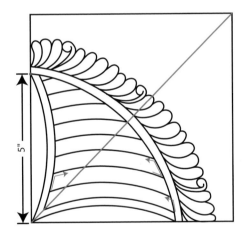

With the feathering complete, we are now ready to stitch ½" curved crosshatching using the 12" arc template. Notice that there is a red marked line drawn 45° from either side. This is a guide so that the crosshatching remains neatly centered. Trace along the inner large arc until the template is in position. Stitch an arc ½" from the inner frame. Continue filling the space with ½" spaced arcs all in one direction.

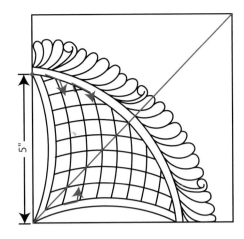

Upon reaching the end of the space, trace along the arc stitching to position the machine to quilt the ½" spaced arcs in the opposite direction. Each arc should cross both the opposite arc as well as the red guide line to ensure that the crosshatch diamonds make a neat line down the center of this space. Properly quilted crosshatching will yield a row of diamonds down the red centerline guide.

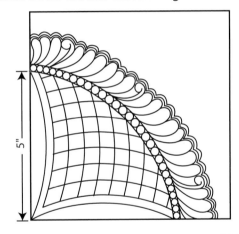

Fill the channel by the feather's spine with pebbles. This creates a nice texture with which to juxtapose both the feathers and the crosshatching. Travel in the seam to the top of the feathers. Stitch two lines of tight echo about ¹⁄₁₆" apart around the perimeter of the feathering. These echo lines help to give definition to the feathers to set them off from the filler that is stitched beyond them. Lastly, if desired, every other space of the crosshatching may be densely filled to create even more definition and texture to the design. ZEN GARDEN was backfilled with lines, but any tight filler will accomplish the same task.

Outer Border

Photo by Jeffrey Lomicka

The quilting of the outer border consists of the appliqué flowers and leaves, and several components quilted into the background. As with the appliqué Tulip Setting Squares, it is best to first ditch stitch all of the appliqué vines, leaves, and flowers. The threads mentioned previously are appropriate in this location too.

I frequently place a stitching pattern of parallel lines at the outer edge of quilts because I believe it tends to draw the viewer's eye outwards. It creates a finishing frame, so to speak. Creating movement of the eye is an important goal of both the piecing AND the quilting. The lines are stitched using a straight longarm template and are spaced ¼" apart. They can be continuously stitched along the border because it is possible to travel along the vine to get to the starting point of the next line. Someone seeking less dense quilting might consider a ½" spacing instead.

Another goal of the quilting was to highlight the small butterflies appliquéd into the background. A set of 6-7 parallel and curving lines stitched with a curved template accomplished this. Each butterfly's path shows distinctly because the parallel line quilting visually disrupts the nondescript background fill that is everywhere else.

The quilting on the appliqué flowers was intended to give texture rather than to appear overly realistic. The main flower motif was outline stitched in coordinating pink and purple InvisaFil threads. The small diamonds were each stitched to create the illusion of tiny petals.

It comes down to personal taste whether or not the appliqué leaves really need to receive detail quilting. The smaller leaves are a nice size to leave alone, but the larger ones, in my opinion, are too large. As a result, each leaf has quilted veining. The central vein was stitched with a large circle template, but the smaller side veins are freehand stitched taking care to neatly backtrack down each line of stitching. A 100 wt. green polyester InvisaFil thread was used, but this detail stitching could have been done with any thread up to a 40 wt. One of the obvious downfalls to quilting veining on every leaf individually was that this required 72 stops and starts! That makes for a whole lot of knotting and burying of thread ends.

A freehand filler is quilted in the tan area of the quilt around the appliqué and star. It is my version of the fill Karen McTavish popularized, combining sections of moving and curving parallel lines with small clusters of pebbles. In reality, any tight fill that you like can be quilted in this space. This fill gives nice movement to the background where the butterflies are flitting around and it is relatively quick to stitch. It is important to quilt this design using a thin thread, 60 wt. or thinner, as areas of backtrack stitching can get thready.

The steps for quilting this pattern are very simple. Find a starting point and stitch a curving, flowy line. You are creating a shape that is nonrigid, almost podlike. The length of these shapes varies, but is on the order of 1½ to 2 inches.

Fill the pod with at least two more parallel curving lines. Try to vary how many lines are placed within each shape as well as the pod's length and width.

Backtrack partly up the outer edge of the pod, and create another pod in a different direction. Fill with lines.

Fill the nook created between these two pods with concentric circles. Some quilters call this a peacock filler. When the circles reach the bottom of the pods, backtrack to another place to start a new pod.

Each time pods are created, fill the new spaces with concentric circles/arcs or a neat patch of pebbles. You will discover that this filler is much simpler to stitch than it is to describe with words!

The Center Star and Outer Star Points

Words about the Lone Star…

Quilts made up of pieced patches always present themselves interestingly. While quilting designed to separately fill each patch is sometimes not the most visually stimulating, occasionally secondary patterns arise that make this a viable way to design. Lone Star or Carpenter's Star quilts are a little different because the patches are too small to quilt something that would be visible in each diamond. For ZEN GARDEN, I chose to create an overlay quilting design for the pieced star. Overlay quilting somewhat ignores the piecing, creating quilting that is different from the piecing yet still able to enhance the piecing. It does, however, use the piecing as a guide. We know that this quilt's star is made up of only diamonds, but in some places the quilting barely shows a hint of a diamond. The gradations of color in the piecing dominate and boldly show that the quilt is a star, so I encourage quilters to take a different approach on the quilting. Let the quilting stand on its own too.

The quilting for the center star is predominantly freehand point-to-point quilting executed with no marking. Green lines show where an interim star has been created within the Lone Star. The meandering green line is freehand (aka eye-balled!) A scalloped motif, shown in pink, is stitched with a 4" circle template. It then receives a ¼" echo, and the resulting space is pebbled. This scalloped-edge rosette softens the strong linear look of the star and immediately draws the viewer's eye right to the center of the quilt.

To stabilize the star, the leaves at the center, shown in blue, should be quilted next. This was done in a dark green 100 wt. thread, which is different from the sage green used on the remainder of the Lone Star, but the same thread could have been used instead. Many of my earlier quilts were less adventurous in their choices of thread.

The last motif to stitch is the feathers, shown here in blue. Because these were quilted in fine thread, I was able to stitch one feather, backtrack down the spine, then quilt another feather. These feathers were quilted completely continuously.

Now the Lone Star is ready for the fillers. These dense designs pop the motifs just stitched. Tight echoing is quilted around the feathers. Eighth-inch spaced lines, shown in yellow, span the space between the feathers and the rosette, while ¼" spaced lines, shown in purple, go between the rosette and the interim star. Take care to aim the lines out the respective star point radially for the greatest effect.

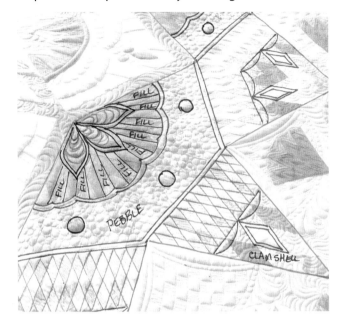

Like the central Lone Star, quilting motifs for the outer star points ignore the diamond piecing and use it only as a guide for the quilting. This is quilted with 100 wt. WonderFil InvisaFil thread in a color coordinating with the fabrics. Begin by stitching in the ditch, shown here in green. Then proceed to the pink lines, which further stabilize the diamond units and break the area up into smaller spaces.

Curved lines are quilted with 4" and 6" circle templates. Next, the petals at the inner point of the diamonds, shown in blue, are stitched. They are filled with concentric arcs, shown in yellow, giving the design immense texture. The rays that span outward of these petals are marked so that there are six spaces per diamond unit. The spacing is eye balled, using the piecing as a guide. Alternating spaces are backfilled with the squiggle line filler shown previously. The space between the scalloped

and straight line frames is pebbled. Three 1" large pebbles are quilted for variety.

The area crosshatched, shown in yellow, simply uses the diamond piecing to space the hatching. Alternating diamonds are also filled with tight lines to create texture. Lastly, the area at the outer reaches of the star points is quilted with a freehand Baptist Fan pattern. This design quilts up tightly and quickly using the steps shown below.

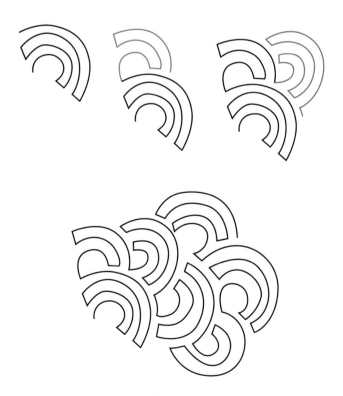

Binding - ZEN GARDEN

While instructions are given for creating and attaching bindings for the quilts in this book, I urge each quilter to take one additional step, something I do for every quilt I make. Using a small quilt sandwich about 8" long and of comparable thickness, create a sample binding. This means you need to use the exact same battings that are in the quilt and quilt it as densely as the edge of your quilt is quilted. As a longarm quilter, I usually have fabric scraps quilted along the side of my actual quilt, scraps that I have used to either test the tension after changing a bobbin or where I test quilt a motif. These scraps are perfect for this. Use this sample to test your method and confirm that the width of binding is correct.

Many factors can affect what binding width is needed, factors including but not limited to the materials of construction, density of stitching at the edge, changes in desired binding width, and whether there is a piping. Don't find out after stitching 250" of binding to the quilt that it is not the desired width, or that when the binding is turned to the backside it does not actually cover the stitching line!

ZEN GARDEN features a very commonly used ⅜" wide, double-fold bias-cut binding made from a cotton quilting fabric. Though the actual quilt has a piping, the following instructions only outline how the binding itself would be made and attached. The quilt requires 275" of binding.

Instructions for Binding

1. Press and starch a 29" square of fabric. Spray it with starch and press a second time. This additional starching helps the bias-cut binding, which will stretch naturally, from being too stretchy.

2. Cut the square into two triangles along a diagonal.

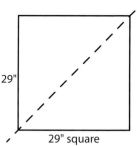

3. Sew the two triangles together to create a rhombus. Use a short stitch length, at least 15 stitches per inch. Press the seam open and trim to ⅛" seam. This will minimize any seam bulk on the finished binding.

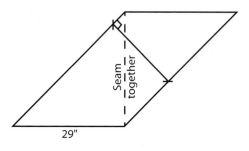

4. Fold the rhombus in half, scantly trim the edge to ensure it is straight, then cut (7) - 2½" strips.

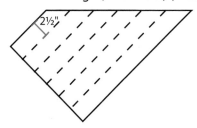

5. Next, the seven binding strips need to be attached to form one continuous strip. Lay two strips right sides up in a straight line end to end along a cutting board line. Overlay the end of one strip of binding (A) on top of the other (B). Be sure to overlap the ends by the width of the strip or more.

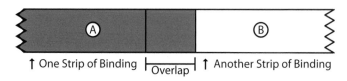

↑ One Strip of Binding ⊢ Overlap ⊣ ↑ Another Strip of Binding

6. Cut a 45° diagonal with a rotary cutter and ruler. It does not matter if the cut is actually 45° since the strips are cut together. The direction of this angular cut should be consistently in the same direction for all joined pieces. It should also match the direction from the existing seam created in step two. While this is not a steadfast requirement of binding construction, it will create a more professional looking finished edge.

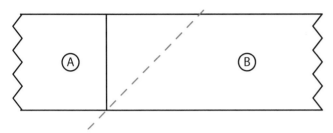

7. Offset strip B from strip A with right sides together, so they match perfectly at the ¼" point.

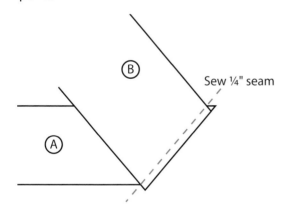

Sew ¼" seam

8. Sew these two strips together using a ¼" seam allowance, and the same short stitch length as previously used. If they are not sewn together now and they get out of order, they will not match perfectly with different strips.

9. Continue attaching the remaining binding strips one at a time using the described method until all strips are joined. This method works whether the binding is straight grain or bias cut.

10. Press the seams open and trim each seam allowance to ⅛".

11. Press the binding in half to form a double-fold binding.

12. Lay the binding around the entire quilt to visually inspect whether a seam in the binding will potentially align with one of the corners. If it does, it is simpler to alter the starting point now to avoid the added bulk at a corner.

13. Adjust the needle position to yield a ⅜" wide seam. Use a normal stitch length to attach the binding.

14. Stitch the binding onto the quilt starting a small distance away from one of the corners leaving a 4" to 5" tail of binding.

15. Stop at a point ⅜" from the bottom edge of the quilt. With needle down, pivot the quilt 45° and stitch directly to the corner. Cut the threads.

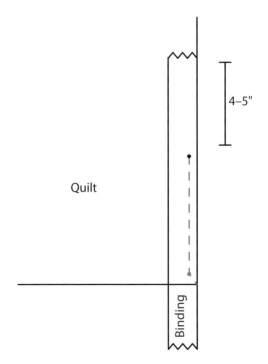

Quilt

Binding

4–5"

16. Rotate the binding 90° along the angled seam just stitched and finger press the angular crease. This will become the miter on the binding seam.

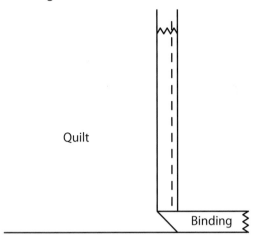

17. Flip the binding 180° so the binding is aligned along the next edge of the quilt. The folded edge of the binding should align exactly with the edge just stitched. Starting at the edge, stitch the next section of binding to the quilt using a ⅜" seam allowance. Continue until 6" to 8" from the starting point.

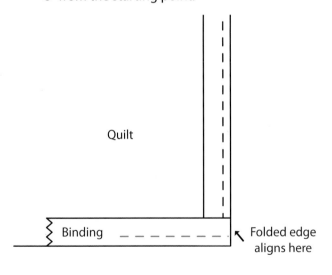

18. Lay the last 6" to 8" of unstitched binding smoothly along the edge of the quilt (B). Place the unstitched binding from the beginning (A) on top of this and mark the angle of the binding's end using chalk or some type of quilt marking pen onto binding part B. The direction of the angle should be consistent with other mitered seams in the binding.

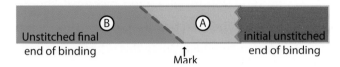

19. Lift binding part A and place a mark ½" to the right of the first marking (you are marking on B). This second mark will be concealed when binding end A is placed back down. This is the line where the binding will be cut. The ½" spacing allows for the width of a seam.

20. Cut binding end B at the second marked line.

21. Pin the two ends together and join with a ¼" seam allowance.

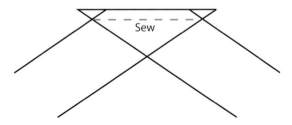

22. Press the seam open, and trim seam allowance to ⅛".

23. Stitch the remaining part of the double-fold binding to the quilt.

24. Turn the binding to the backside and hand stitch.

When hand stitching a binding to the backside of a quilt, select a thread that best matches the color of the binding. I typically use fine polyester thread 60-100 wt. but a 50 wt. cotton also makes a nice finish. The fine threads blend, making the stitches essentially invisible. Stitch with a single strand of thread only. It is a fallacy that doubling the strands of thread will yield a much stronger binding. It will simply make the line of hand stitching show! What makes a strong binding is a tight seam made from closely spaced stitches.

The binding is attached with a ladder stitch. Stitches are placed approximately 10-12 per inch, or more if the binding does not appear to lie smoothly at this interface. Every couple of inches, I tie a knot and bury it along the path of stitching. This also ensures that the binding stitches will not pull out or pull loose. My heavy-use home quilts use this same technique and I have never once had to repair a binding!

Ladder Stitch Instructions

Using a thread that closely matches the binding, bring up the thread in the outermost edge of the binding fold. The knot will be buried in the quilt sandwich. Note that my photo uses a black thread to increase visibility, but this would not be the suggested color for this binding.

Poke the needle into the quilt just beside the binding and immediately adjacent to where it is shown. In a flowing stitch, traverse within the quilt sandwich a short distance (under ⅛"), coming out of the quilt and into the outermost edge of the binding. Tighten the stitch, and repeat. Every few inches, a knot can be placed near the quilt/binding, which is then slipped gently into the quilt sandwich. This knot helps to maintain the integrity of the stitches should the binding be pulled or tugged on. The stitch is called a Ladder Stitch because if you could see the stitches within the quilt, they are short and perpendicular, like the steps on a ladder.

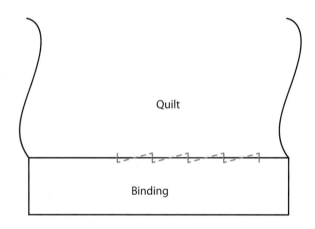

AUTUMN'S SURRENDER

57" x 57"

Inspiration, Design Process, and Finishing

AUTUMN'S SURRENDER was most definitely the start of my love affair with silk. It started with three half yard bundles of Kaufman Silk Radiance I ordered from an online shop where they were on sale for $5 per yard! Not wanting to pass up a bargain, I chose a bundle in three different colorways. I didn't even stop long enough to realize that these were very different colors for me.

I did not have the faintest idea what I was going to make but, was lured by the gorgeous colors and irresistible sheen.

Two years before I started AUTUMN'S SURRENDER, I quilted on Silk Radiance. It was a small wholecloth quilt, which to this day is neither bound nor completed! Quilting on silk was captivating, but every detail of the quilting design was illuminated via this glorious fabric. I wanted to try again.

I entered into this project without a plan, unlike how I had approached several other quilts preceding AUTUMN'S SURRENDER. At that point in my quilting, I often had much of the quilt designed on EQ7 software prior to buying or cutting fabric. I used the software to help me choose colors and tweak the quilt blocks or layout.

A wise quilter might first try piecing this fabric to test its user friendliness. Not me. I drafted a design

that had a free pieced tree-like center (dare I call the piecing modern?), lots of Flying Geese, and a border of quarter circle blocks similar to those that are used to create the Winding Ways or Drunkard's Path pattern. The latter were the blocks I decided to piece first. They were relatively small, maybe 3" - 4" square. I patiently made at least a dozen of these before I bravely took a step back, realizing that this design did not stand a chance of working out well. The curved seams puckered and the blocks looked horrible.

In the first version of the Radiance quilt, the silk was not interfaced. The curved piecing was slippery and challenging to stitch smoothly. I knew that these blocks were not going to yield a quilt that I would want to finish, let alone compete. I hate admitting defeat and having to come up with an alternate plan. The reality is that this is an everyday occurrence in this business. It is how we learn, and how I have amassed an incredible foundation of skills that help me make beautiful and successful quilts. It was time for Plan B.

My experiences with the silk led me to the conclusion that it would not piece smoothly, and it might be easier to avoid curved seams. Interfacing the silk would provide added stability and inhibit raveling, I went back to the drawing board with a few main goals: simplify the design, keep the pieces a reasonable size, and avoid curved piecing.

The Plan B design was significantly different from where this quilt began. Though still a medallion quilt, the geese were gone and it was noticeably simpler. The yardage of silk was interfaced prior to cutting pieces with Pellon® Bi-Stretch Lite™, a very lightweight tricot-style fusible interfacing. I was reluctant to interface the silk because so many fusibles make the fabric stiff and incapable of showing the quilting details. The Pellon interfacing was perfect. The silk still felt soft and pliable, just a smidge thicker than initially.

The design underwent a couple more significant changes in its evolution from initial concept to what was to be pieced as AUTUMN'S SURRENDER. Most notably was the elimination of the deep peacock blue fabric. There was not enough deep blue material left after my initial curved piecing fiasco for the outer border, and at the time I was not interested in buying more.

The most challenging part of developing the pattern turned out not to be making something out of the finicky silk fabric, but rather staying true to my own personal design aesthetic. I strongly believe that quilts that are characteristic of a quilter's personal style are simpler to make, and will inevitably show more of the quilter's best features.

I struggled getting the many colors of fabric to play cohesively. Brown and blue are two colors that I would not typically select for a quilt, yet I had a pile of browns and a pile of blues! I asked myself on many occasions what was I doing and why I purchased colors uncharacteristic of me.

The solution was really quite simple. My aesthetic needed the greens to be front and center. This is a color I gravitate toward and wanted as the focus of the quilt.

The many shades of pale blue were used as the background. As I was piecing this background, it felt a little scrappy which was not really my intention, but I was confident I could bring the many shades together with the quilting.

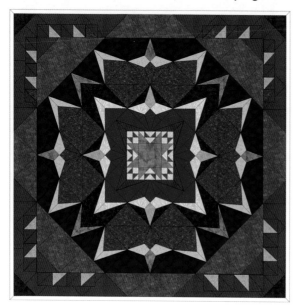

Sadly, even experienced quilters have the joy of learning things in hindsight, more often than many think. With the design finished and much of the quilt pieced, I still struggled with how simple the quilt seemed compared to my other competition quilts. I had it in my head that I needed more piecing. When I got to the borders of the design, I chose to deviate from the plan. I pieced a crazy striped contraption of golds and browns instead. It looked absolutely horrible, only exacerbated by my severe dislike of brown!

Since creating this quilt and competing at nearly a dozen shows, I can honestly say I have never read a judge's critique stating the piecing was too simple. On the contrary, the very simple piecing with the showy fabrics creates an ideal backdrop letting the classic quilting shine. The lesson here is to give the quilt top only what it needs. Overwhelming the quilt with piecing takes away from something else.

Despite this being a rather simply pieced quilt, intersections where more than six points came together were not lying correctly. The points did not all meet accurately. The culprit was the increased thickness of the interfaced silk. The interfacing complicated my ability to be accurate. As a quilter who routinely puts quilts under the constant critique of judges, I knew that the quilt would not be competitive unless I fixed these points.

I knew I needed to find a way to cover these inexact intersections. My solution was to create a diamond appliqué. Little did I know that this would actually become part of the design! Appliqués were hand stitched over more than the few offending intersections. I put twenty of them onto the quilt top. The bulky misaligned joints were then cut away from the top so that the bulk would not cause the appliqué to look lumpy. This is my typical treatment for appliqués if there are any seams beneath them. The net effect of adding the appliqués to the top was most definitely a positive. They add to the autumn-to-winter theme, giving the illusion of a snowflake.

I frequently begin designing the quilting before the top is entirely pieced. I use a number of different techniques for envisioning motifs from high tech electronic drawing to down and dirty drawing on printed photographs. There are quilts and instances when one works better than another. For AUTUMN'S SURRENDER, I initially sketched some ideas on a printed EQ7 rendition of the quilt top. This is often how I jot down my first ideas for the quilting.

I wanted the quilting to share the symmetrical appearance of the top. Motifs designed for one side of the quilt would be repeated on the other three sides. The simplest way to identically make this happen is to create a template or to pre-mark the top with the design using a light box. I planned to do the latter, at least in the sections of lighter colors.

When creating actual size templates or patterns, I frequently use tracing paper. Many sheets are taped together, then placed on top of the quilt. With a pencil, and using immense care, I trace the shape of the section I want to design. Once the boundaries for the quilting are drawn, I take the tracing paper off the quilt, and sketch the design.

This method proved very helpful when drawing motifs for the scrappy pieced pale blue background, as the shape was irregular and I wanted the quilting to transcend the boundaries of the color changes. Most importantly, though, it allowed me to generate quilting that was actual size, so I knew precisely how it would look and fit in the space. I used this technique on other areas of the quilt as well.

I frequently get questions from quilters at shows about how I mark the top prior to quilting. I am a

freehand quilter, not having a computer automated longarm machine, so everything that is stitched is done one motif at a time. Unless the quilt is a wholecloth, where I demand exact symmetry, I absolutely will not trace an entire design onto a quilt. It is tedious and a ridiculous waste of time. It is only necessary to mark the outline of key shapes that the eye will discern as different if they are not marked. As an example, on the pale blue background area, I only marked the spines for the feathers. As I quilt, I make note of where the leaves were interspersed into the feathers so that they are consistently in the same places. Similarly, I try to keep track of approximate numbers of feathers and locations of curls, especially when they are in places where the lack of symmetry would be highly visible. The reality is that I do not want my quilting to look like a machine executed it. The natural variations are beautiful.

Reasons for selecting a particular thread for a certain quilt all stem from personal choice. Any thread will work, but some are clearly better alternatives than others. Assuming the quilt is uniformly quilted, the thread selected will affect the visual appeal of the quilt. AUTUMN'S SURRENDER is made from high sheen, solid showy fabrics. I wanted the thread to yield luscious texture but not overwhelm the delicate material and design. Silk 100 wt. was the perfect choice. It has a luster similar to the fabric, and is so fine that it nearly melts into the fabric when stitched. This fine thread allows for ultra-dense stitching without so much as the appearance of thread buildup.

It is fairly typical for me to finish a project and think that a different thread may have yielded a better or more desired look. These lessons come with every completed quilt, so I have become accustomed to no longer being frustrated. What might I have done differently on AUTUMN'S SURRENDER? I would perhaps use a heavier weight (40-50 wt.) thread with a sheen to stitch feather motifs and to outline larger key designs. Silk 100 wt. is fantastic for dense stitching, but feature designs could stand to be a little more prominent.

Creating cohesion with quilting may appear to involve magic, but following a few simple guidelines

makes all the difference. Let me share how this was done with AUTUMN'S SURRENDER.

- *Allow the essence of the piecing or the theme of the quilt to be apparent in the quilting.* At the time I was quilting this, I may not have had the AUTUMN'S SURRENDER name, but the colors in the quilt reminded me of fall. I wanted to keep the quilting more organic, hence the leaves interspersed in the feathers.

- *Utilize a good mixture of flowy designs with more structured designs.* Crosshatching and parallel lines are more rigid and do an excellent job of juxtaposing the more flowy designs. These designs, additionally, can create beautiful frames for other quilting or a finished edge on the quilt, as is seen with the brown octagon.

- *Repeating motifs help to create cohesion.* AUTUMN'S SURRENDER has two sections of flowing feathers, in the chartreuse medallion and in the pale blue background. There are numerous sections of crosshatching. The density and the style of crosshatching was altered to create variety, but the mere repetition of a similar design creates unity. The circle motif is used in a variety of places and in a variety of sizes. The two chartreuse sections both share a similar scrolling design.

- *Bring a motif of the piecing into the quilting.* The 2" inner green border brings the diamond design from the appliqué into the quilting.

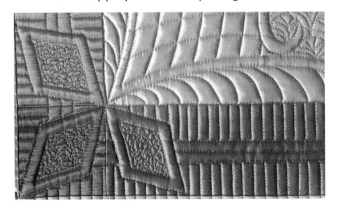

Many professional quilters strongly suggest using a heavily printed fabric for the backing. A print will hide any obvious errors like tension anomalies, or missed back tracking. For this quilt, I wanted a more dramatic effect.

I chose a solid taupe cotton sateen for the backing which would allow all the quilting efforts to shine. This choice of fabric, in effect, creates a dual-sided quilt. While the cotton sateen is a beautiful fabric, the inherent weave of this fabric makes it challenging, if not impossible, to unpick stitches. Anything unstitched was done from the front.

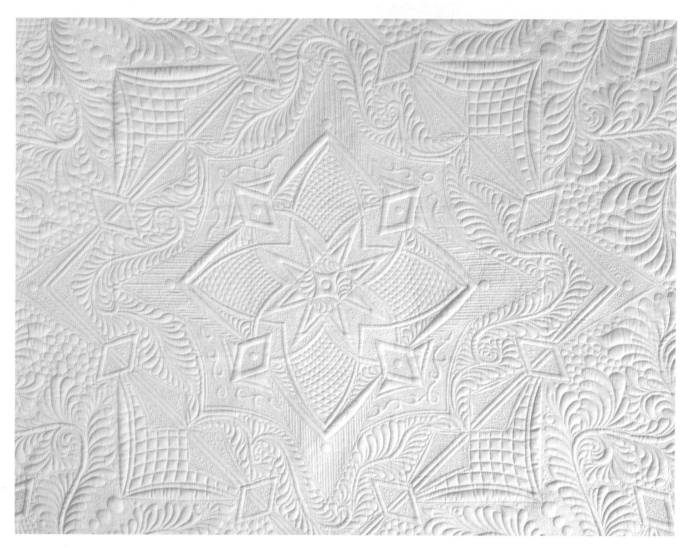

Awards

Best Wall Quilt, AQS Des Moines, 2015

Best Frame Machine Quilting, MQX New England, 2014

Exceptional Merit, Vermont Quilt Festival, 2014

1st Place, Minnesota Quilt Show, 2016

1st Place, MQX New England, 2014

1st Place, Road to California, 2015

1st Place, AQS Paducah, 2015

1st Place, Shipshewana Quilt Festival, 2015

1st Place, AQS Chattanooga, 2015

2nd Place, Quilt Odyssey, 2014

2nd Place, AQS Daytona, 2016

3rd Place, Quiltfest Mid-Atlantic Show, 2014

3rd Place, IQF World of Beauty, Houston, 2014

3rd Place, Wisconsin Quilt Show, 2016

HM, Indiana Heritage Quilt Festival, 2015

Fabric Requirements

Color	Yardage	Location
Orange 1	⅜	A, I, H
Orange 2 (little deeper)	⅛	A, J
Gold	¼	B, 4 diamonds
Silvery gray	½	A, B, C
Chartreuse	⅝	B, C, D, O
Pale sky blue	½	C, K
Sky blue	1¼	D, E, F, M, N, P, R
Blue	⅝	G, H, I
Slate	1¼	K, S, outer border
Grass	¾	C, D, inner border
Forest	⅛	8 diamonds, inner border cornerstones
Rust	⅛	8 diamonds, (8) ½" dots
Brown	1⅝*	H, I, J, K, L, binding
Backing	2 for wide, 4 for 40"	
⁵⁄₁₆" Rust velvet ribbon	5	Trim
Interfacing	17	

*fabric includes ½" wide binding not cut on the bias.

Assembly Diagram

Approximately 60" x 60"

Using Silk Radiance

AUTUMN'S SURRENDER is made from Kaufman's Silk Radiance.

Some of the deeper colors have bled for me. As a rule, I soak every material darker than ivory in very hot water to test for color fastness. I never use Retayne™ Color Fixative, as I don't know what the chemicals will do to the sheen of the silk.

Silk dye lots can vary slightly. Purchase all you need of a single color at once.

Interface with Pellon Bi-Stretch Lite to stabilize the silk and inhibit raveling. It comes 20" wide so 17 yards is needed to interface the silk for this quilt. Interfacing can be purchased by the 10-yard bolt.

I don't suggest using a commercial dryer to dry Radiance. There are reports that it dulls the sheen of the silk. Lay it flat on towels to dry.

Paper Pieced Templates

This quilt is mostly paper pieced, take care that all of the outer edges of the block are on the grain.

Star A

Finished Size 6½" x 6½". Make 1.

Paper Piecing Pattern on page 71.

Templates on pages 77–78.

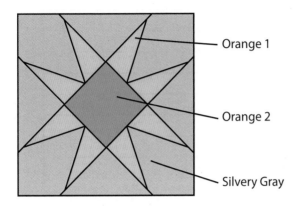

Orange 1

Orange 2

Silvery Gray

Arrow B

Finished size 6½" x 6½". Make 4.

Paper Piecing Pattern on page 72.

Template on page 79.

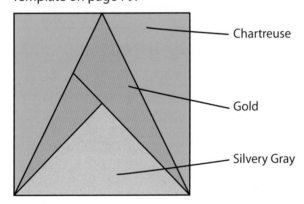

Chartreuse

Gold

Silvery Gray

Kites C

Finished size 6½" x 6½". Make 4

Paper Piecing Pattern on page 73.

Templates on pages 80.

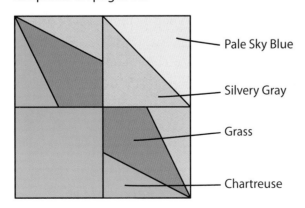

Pale Sky Blue

Silvery Gray

Grass

Chartreuse

Arrow D

Finished size 6½" x 6½". Make 4

Paper Piecing Pattern on page 75.

Templates on pages 81–82.

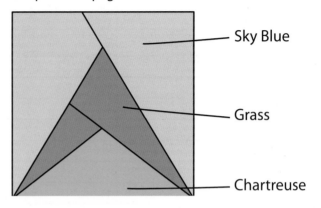

Sky Blue

Grass

Chartreuse

Setting Triangles E

Setting triangles for center 28" square on point

Need 8 triangles.

Cut (2) 10¹³⁄₁₆" x 10¹³⁄₁₆" sky blue squares. Cut diagonally twice.

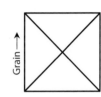

Setting Triangle F

Corner triangles for corners of 28" square on point

Need 4 triangles.

Cut (2) 5½" x 5½" sky blue squares. Cut diagonally.

Center Block Border G

Border of 28" center block

Cut (4) 4" x 21½" blue rectangles.

Brown Setting Triangles L

Need 8 triangles.

Cut (2) 11³⁄₁₆" x 11³⁄₁₆" brown squares. Cut diagonally twice.

Ray I

Make 4.

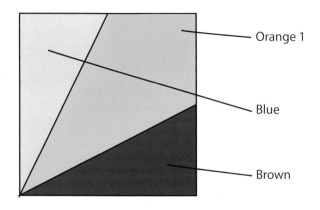

Orange 1

Blue

Brown

Ray J

Make 4.

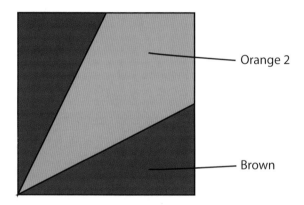

Orange 2

Brown

Ray H

Make 4.

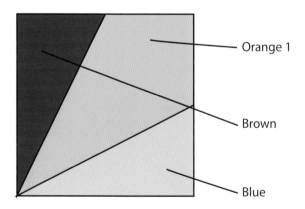

Orange 1

Brown

Blue

Rays H, I, and J Templates on pages 83. All have a finished size of 3½" x 3½". Paper Piecing Pattern on page 74.

Arrow K

Finished size 7" x 7". Make 12.

Paper Piecing Pattern on page76.

Templates on pages 84–85.

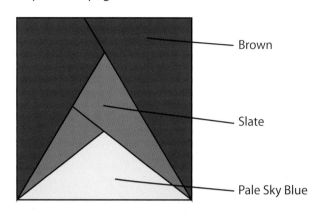

Brown

Slate

Pale Sky Blue

Trapezoid Units

Trapezoid M-O-N. Make 4.

M Template on page 86 . N is the reverse of M.

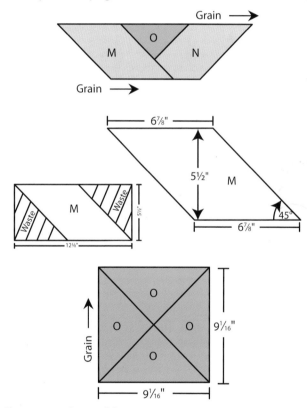

Chartreuse Assembly:

Right sides together.

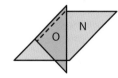

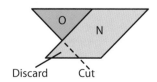

Discard   Cut

Press the seams toward N.

Sew on M.

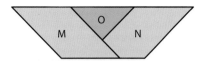

Press seams toward M.

Trapezoid P-O-R-S

Make 4.

P Template on page 87 . R is the reverse of P.

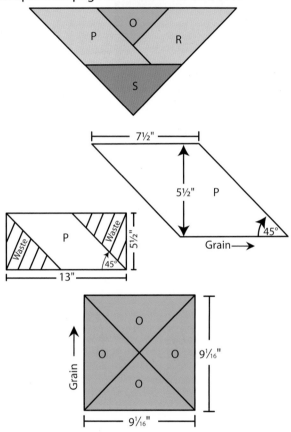

Chartreuse

Refer to instructions for assembly M-N-O when stitching.

Cut (2) 8⁷⁄₁₆" x 8⁷⁄₁₆" slate squares.
Cut diagonally.

Attach S to P-O-R. Press seams toward S.

Note: The color of pieces P and R are the same as for pieces E and F.

Inner Border (Grass and Forest)

For T – Cut (8) 2½" x 29" strips from the grass fabric.

For U – Cut (4) 2½" x 2½" squares from the forest fabric. Angled ends will be cut later.

Stitch U to T. Press the seams toward T. Repeat this process to make 4.

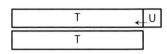

Outer Border (Slate)

Cut long border or binding strips before any other pieces are cut.

Cut (8) 3¾" x 27" strips from the slate fabric. Do not cut 45° miters at this point.

Piecing Directions

Piece the center block sections first in rows as shown below, then attach the columns into a square. Because setting triangles E and F are oversized, the center block will need to be trimmed to 28½" on each side.

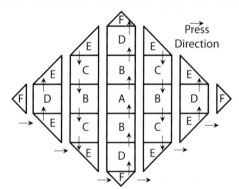

Piece the units as shown above and attach them to the center first attaching 1 and 2, then 3 and 4. Press the seams outward toward G.

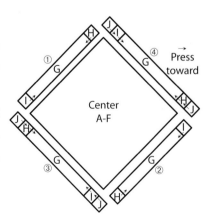

Make 4 units as shown below from K and L pieces.

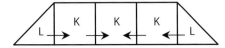

The intersection at the top edge of K will be bulky. If possible, press to one side. Remember, an appliqué and diamond will cover this intersection later.

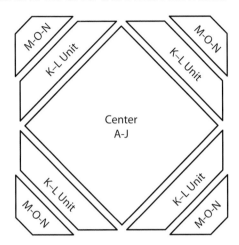

Attach K-L units to the center. Press outwards.

Attach M-O-N units to the 4 sides of the octagon where the K-L triangles are located. Press the seams toward the M-O-N units.

Constructing the Corner Units
(P-O-R-S and two borders)

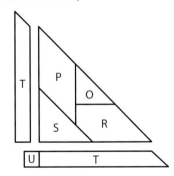

Sew T border to P-O-R-S unit. Press the seams toward T.

Sew T-U onto the corner. Press the seams outward toward T. Do not trim the excess off T.

Adding the Outer Border

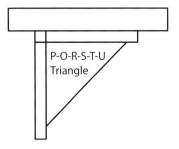

The slate strip is oversized intentionally. Sew on one outer border, making sure to stop the stitching at the left corner ¼" from the edge of the cornerstone. Backstitch 2-3 stitches to keep this from pulling out.

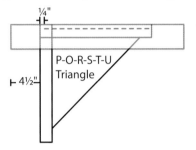

The border should be 4½" beyond the left side. Press the seams toward the outer border.

Attach the other slate outer border exactly the same way.

Create the 45° miter by folding the excess fabric of one V border so it lies on top of the other. Pin the angle and check with a rotary cutting guide, adjusting as needed. The miter should be perfectly along the 45° and the corner should be square. When perfect, press the miter. Hand stitch or glue baste with three to four tiny drops of clear glue and heat set with an iron, then turn to the backside of the fabric and machine stitch along the crease. Trim away excess fabric.

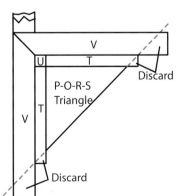

Using a rotary mat and cutting guide, carefully trim excess from the borders as shown.

Stitch the corner units onto the quilt. Press toward the corner.

If you use a velvet trim, add after quilting. The quilt will need to be blocked and you don't want to wet the velvet. Machine or hand appliquéd ¼" bias trim around the outer border of the brown octagon. Use ½" circles to conceal the bias trim ends.

Trim

A ⁵⁄₁₆" rust velvet ribbon trim is hand appliquéd around the octagonal brown border requiring 5 yards.

It is hand stitched in eight separate pieces and the end joints are concealed with a ½" matching circle.

To appliqué the trim perfectly straight, glue baste it into position with clear Elmer's® Glue, hold with vertically placed pins until the ribbon is dry, and then hand stitch.

The ends are treated with No-Fray liquid to keep them from raveling until the ends are covered with rust dots.

Rather than use velvet trim that is not washable, substitute ¼" bias piping. This requires ½ yard of fabric for there to be no seams.

The dots finish at ½" diameter. I used Karen K. Buckley's technique with her Templar circles. Cut circles from the fabric. No interfacing was used on the silk for the rust dots. For detailed instruction, refer to Preparing Turned Edge Circles on page 158.

Diamond Appliqué

Cut fabric about ¼" larger on all sides so the edges may be turned under. You'll need 4 gold, 8 forest, and 8 rust diamonds.

These are turned edge. I made them using two layers of freezer paper, which is pressed to the backside of the fabric. Using a glue stick, secure appliqué seam allowances. The actual diamond is cut approximately ¼" larger than the freezer paper template below.

Hand or machine appliqué the diamonds to the quilt top. The appliqués were a cover up of sorts which turned into a good design decision. From the backside, carefully clip behind the diamond. Trim the quilt top to about ⅜" seam allowance behind the diamond, thereby removing all the bulk.

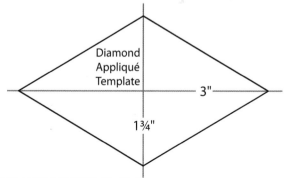

Diamond Appliqué Template — 3" — 1¾"

Star A Paper Piecing Pattern

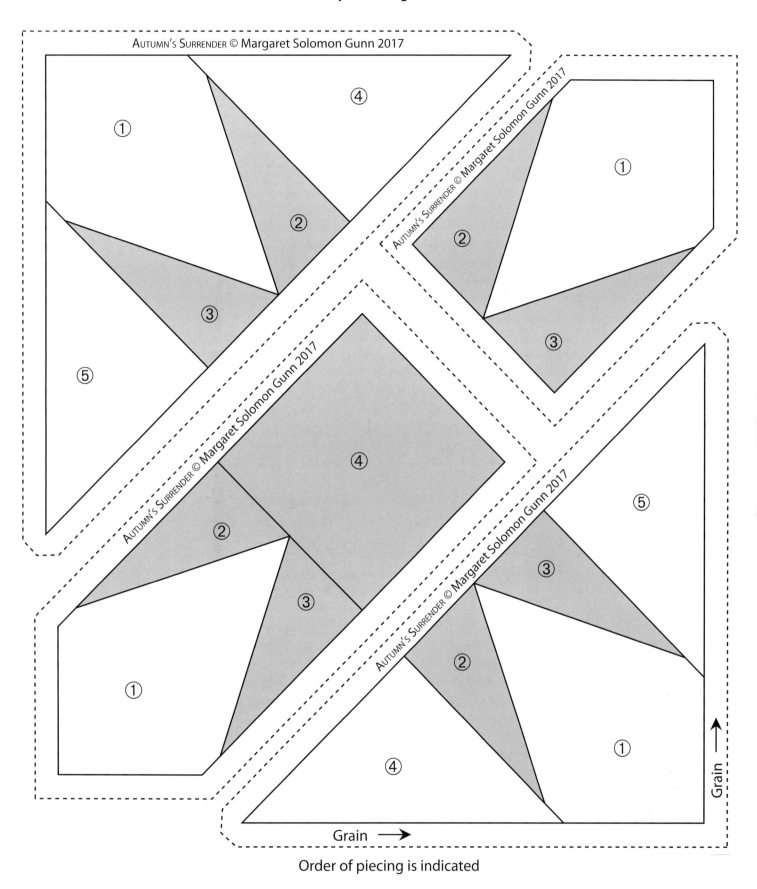

Order of piecing is indicated

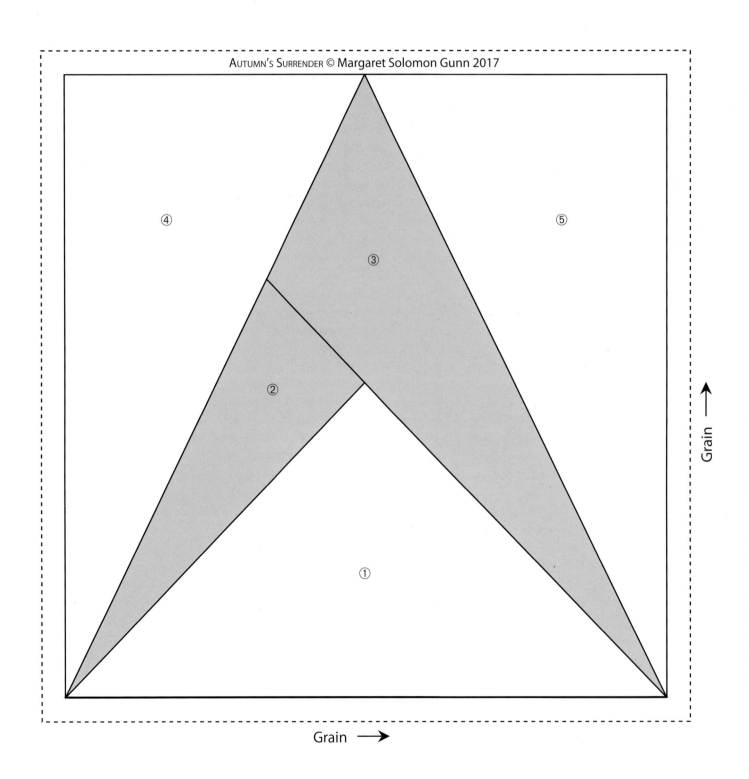

AUTUMN'S SURRENDER © Margaret Solomon Gunn 2017

Grain →

Grain →

Kites C Paper Piecing Pattern

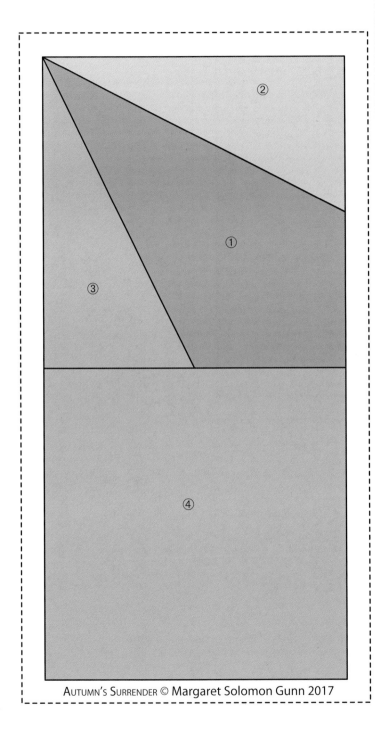

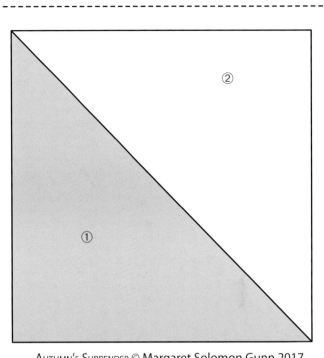

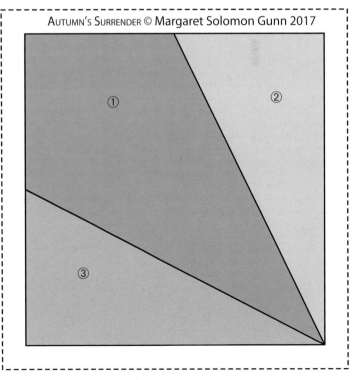

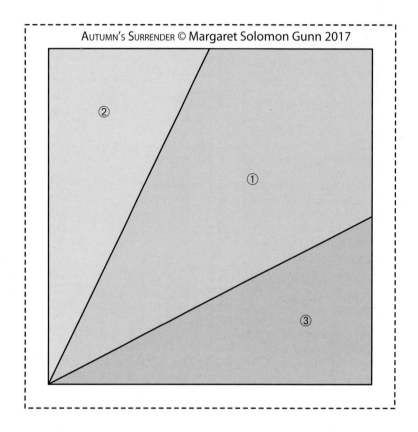

AUTUMN'S SURRENDER © Margaret Solomon Gunn 2017

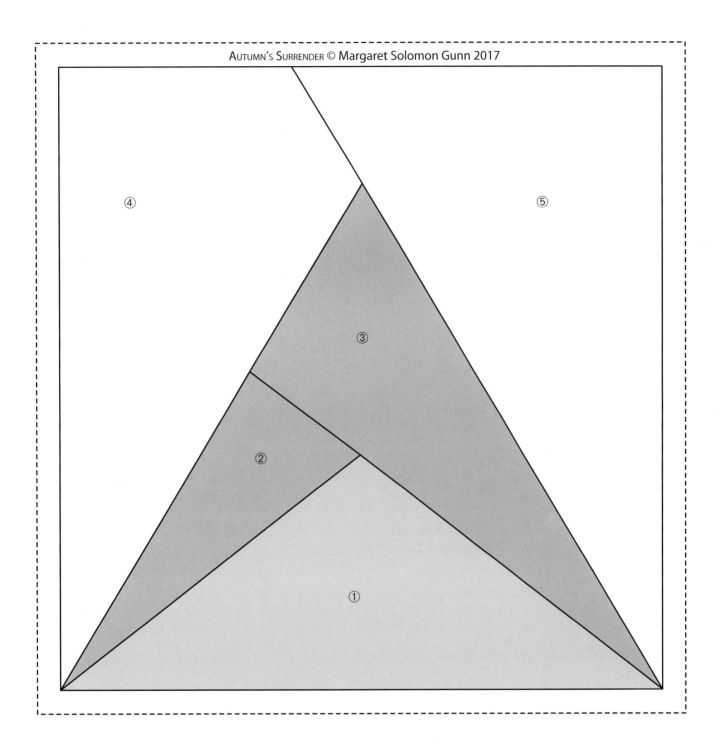

AUTUMN'S SURRENDER © Margaret Solomon Gunn 2017

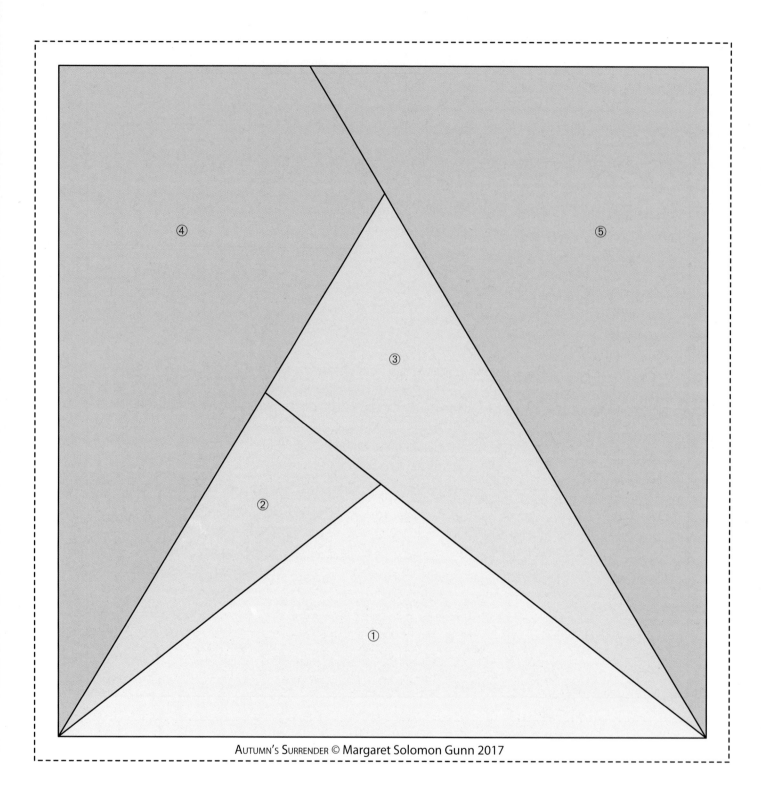

AUTUMN'S SURRENDER © Margaret Solomon Gunn 2017

Star A Templates

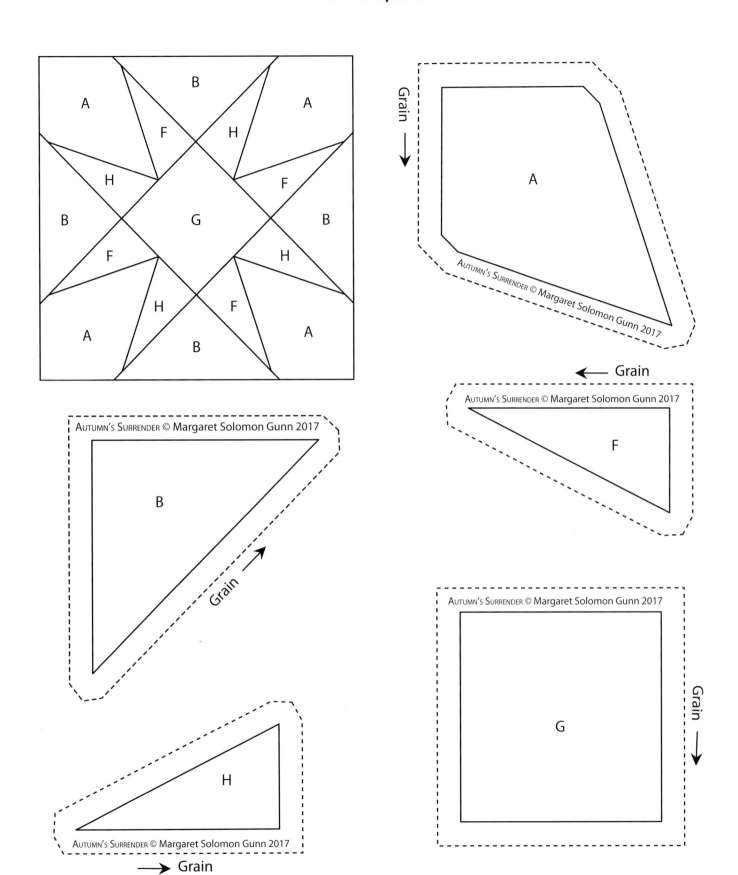

Grain

A

Autumn's Surrender © Margaret Solomon Gunn 2017

← Grain

Autumn's Surrender © Margaret Solomon Gunn 2017

F

Autumn's Surrender © Margaret Solomon Gunn 2017

B

Grain →

Grain

G

H

Autumn's Surrender © Margaret Solomon Gunn 2017

→ Grain

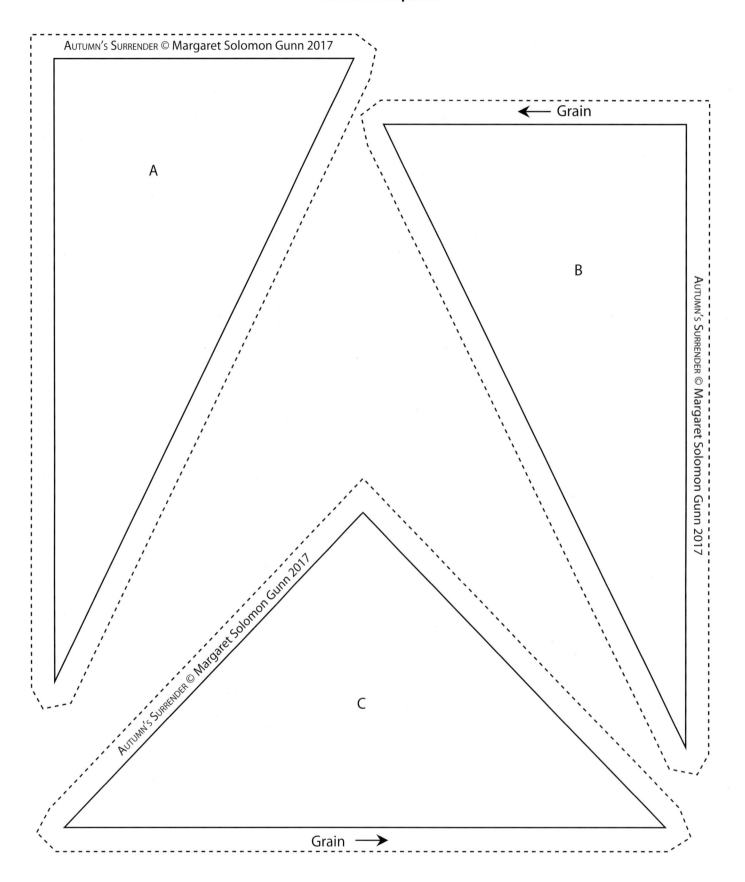

A

Autumn's Surrender © Margaret Solomon Gunn 2017

Grain ←

B

Autumn's Surrender © Margaret Solomon Gunn 2017

Autumn's Surrender © Margaret Solomon Gunn 2017

C

Grain →

Arrow B Templates

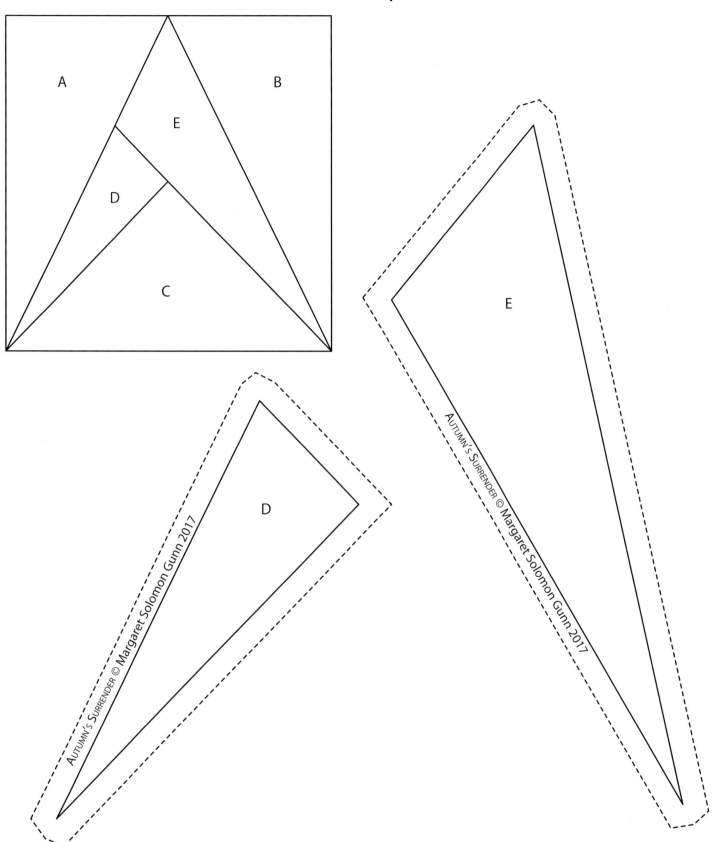

A

B

E

D

C

E

D

Autumn's Surrender © Margaret Solomon Gunn 2017

Autumn's Surrender © Margaret Solomon Gunn 2017

Kites C Templates

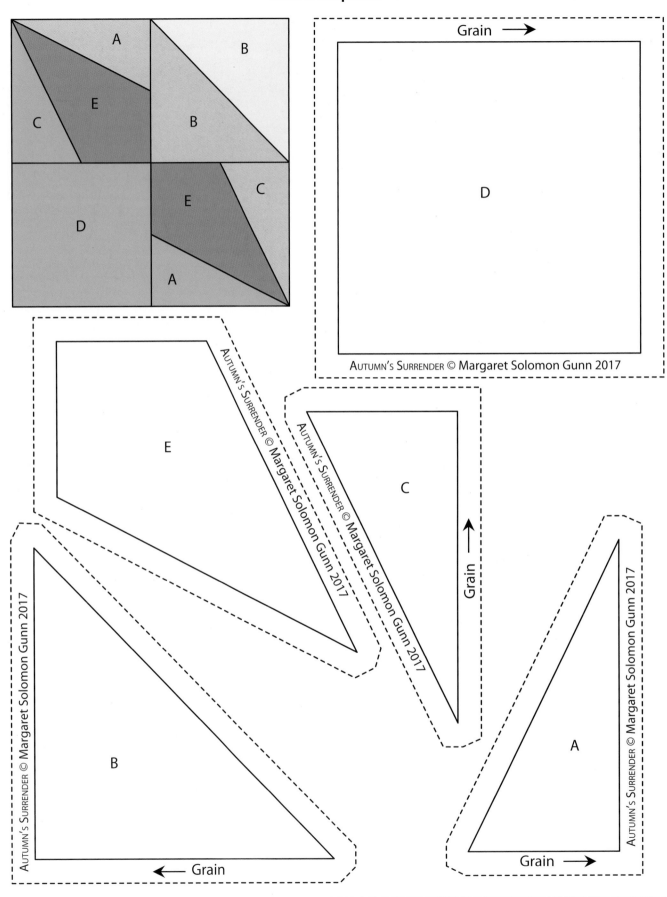

Grain →

A

B

B

E

C

D

E

C

A

D

E

C

Grain ↑

B

A

← Grain

Grain →

Arrow D Templates

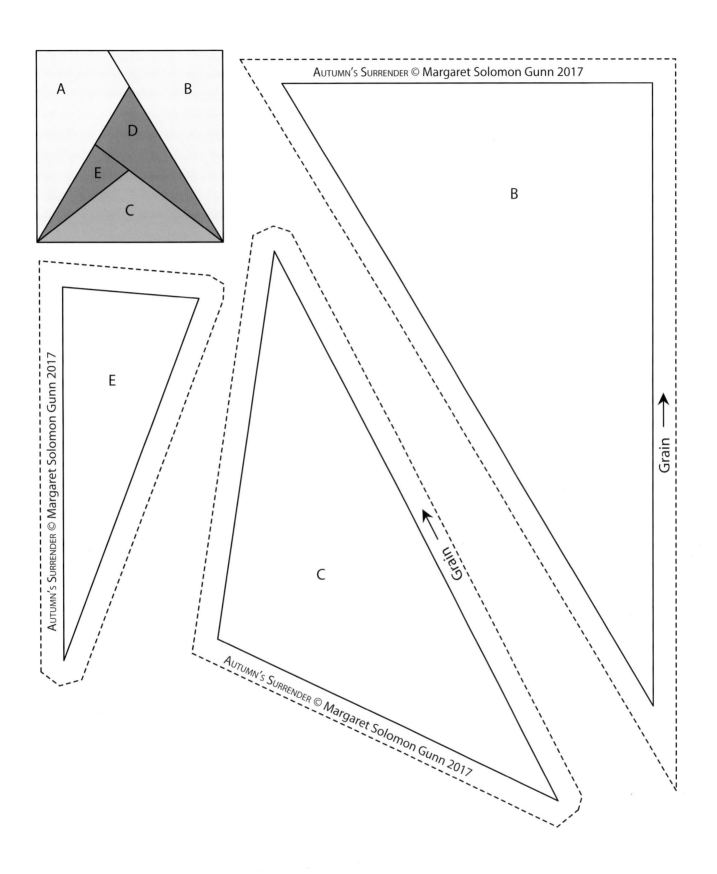

A

B

D

E

C

AUTUMN'S SURRENDER © Margaret Solomon Gunn 2017

B

Grain

AUTUMN'S SURRENDER © Margaret Solomon Gunn 2017

E

Grain

C

AUTUMN'S SURRENDER © Margaret Solomon Gunn 2017

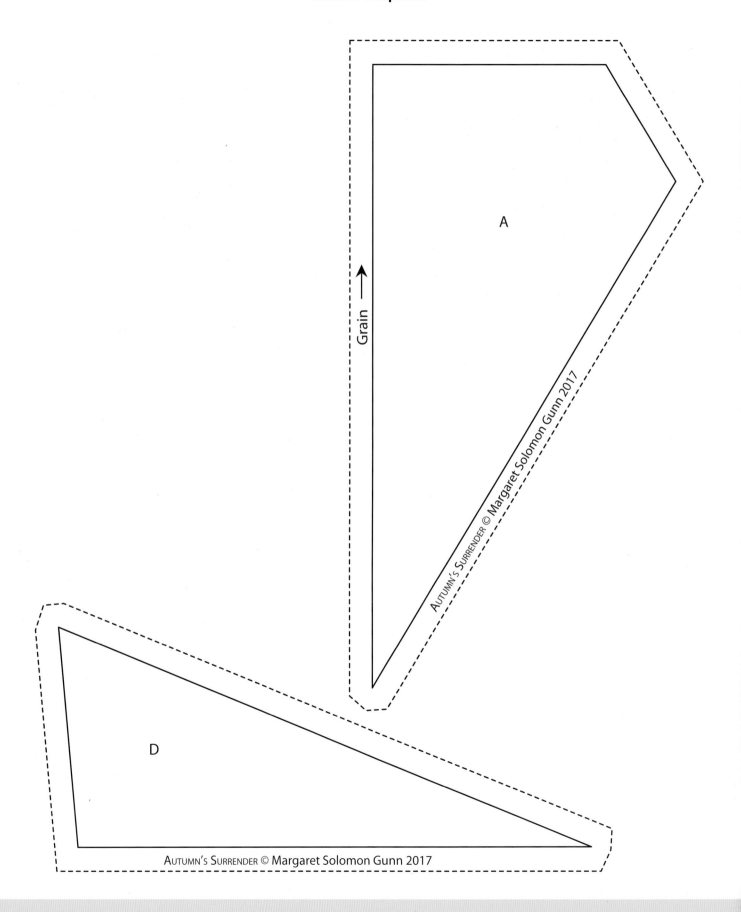

A

Grain →

AUTUMN'S SURRENDER © Margaret Solomon Gunn 2017

D

AUTUMN'S SURRENDER © Margaret Solomon Gunn 2017

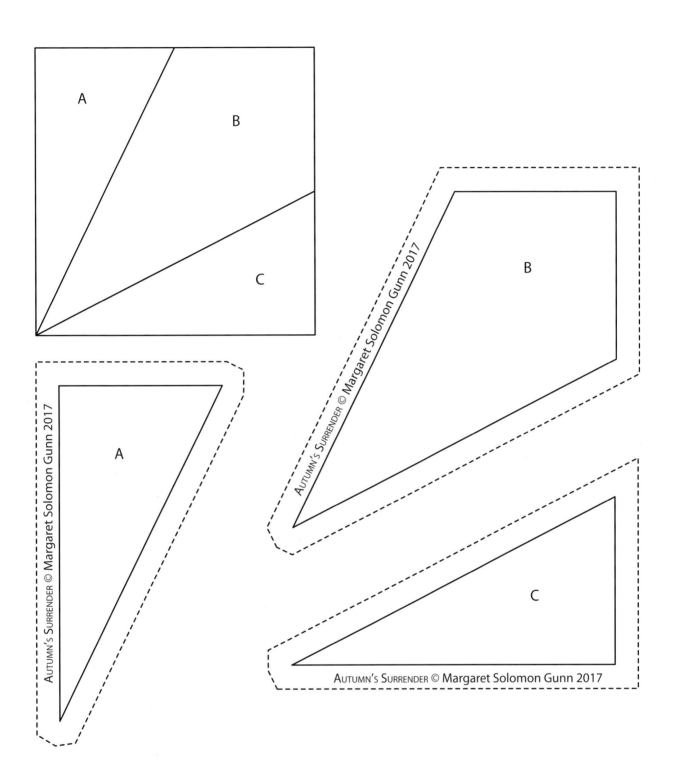

A

B

C

B

C

A

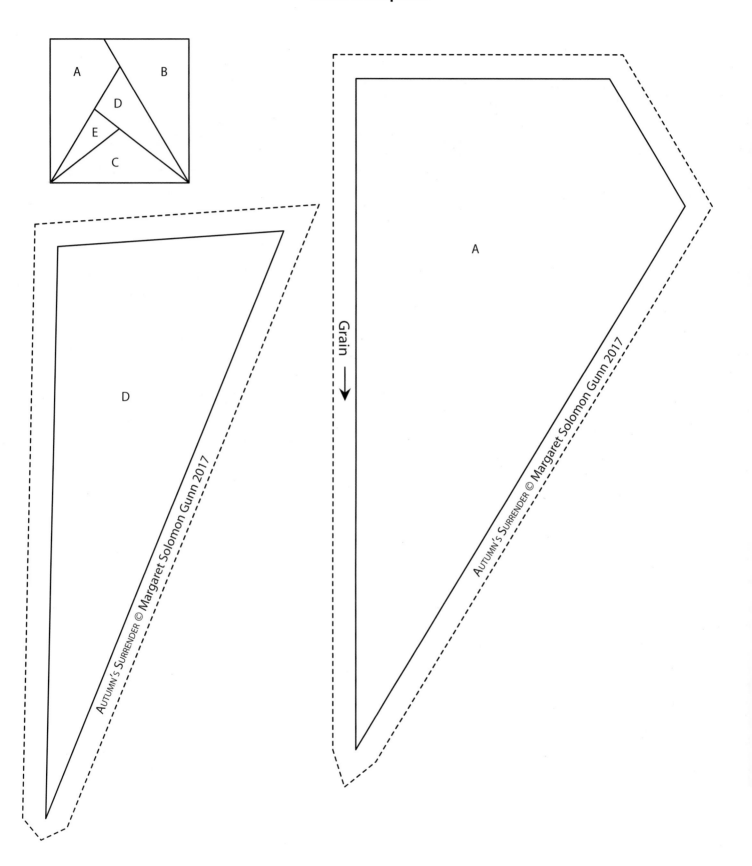

A

B

D

E

C

D

Grain

A

AUTUMN'S SURRENDER © Margaret Solomon Gunn 2017

AUTUMN'S SURRENDER © Margaret Solomon Gunn 2017

Arrow K Templates

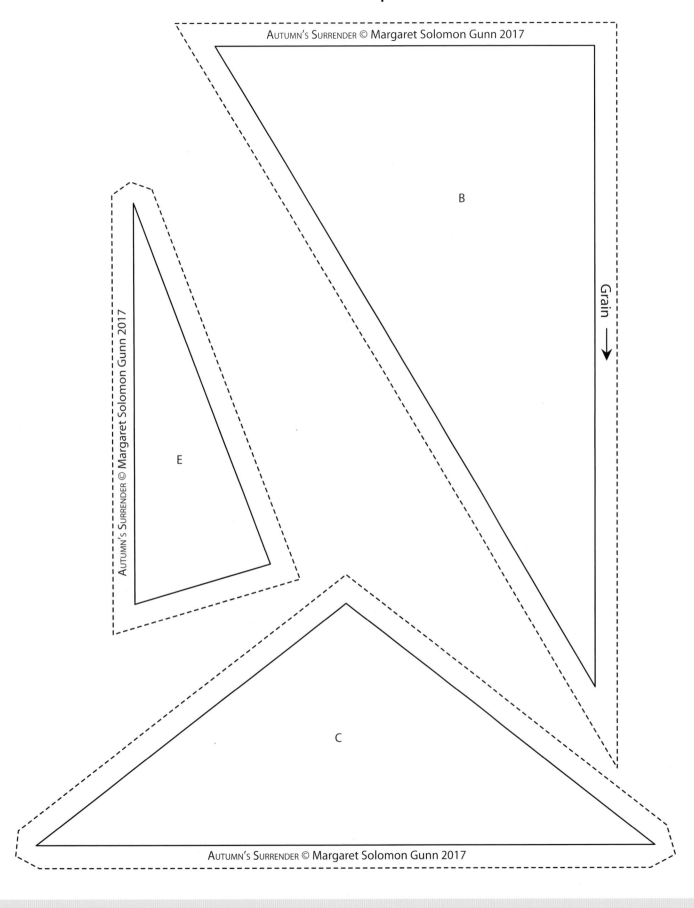

Autumn's Surrender © Margaret Solomon Gunn 2017

B

Grain →

Autumn's Surrender © Margaret Solomon Gunn 2017

E

C

Autumn's Surrender © Margaret Solomon Gunn 2017

Template M

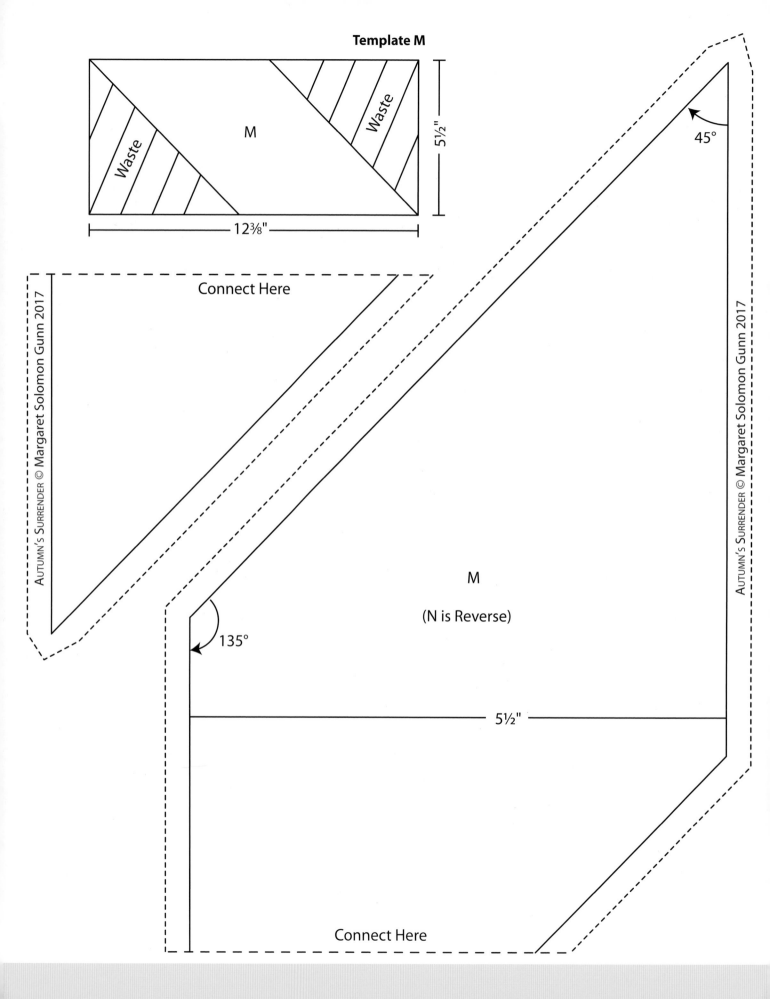

Waste

Waste

M

5½"

12⅜"

45°

135°

M

(N is Reverse)

5½"

Connect Here

Connect Here

Template P

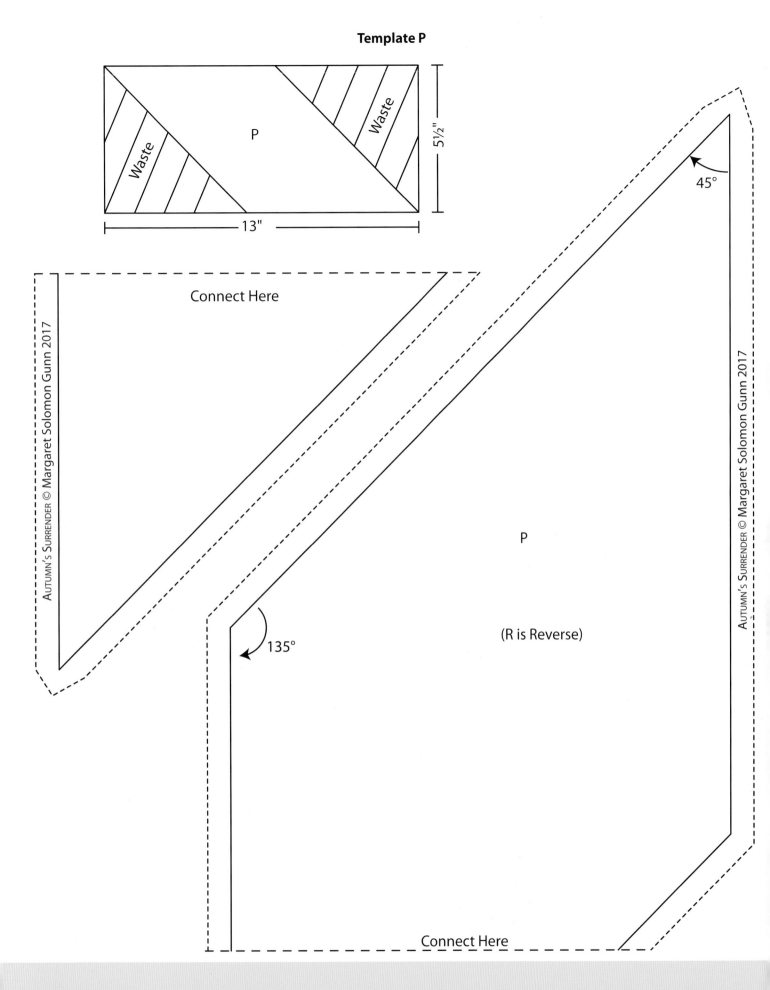

P

Waste

Waste

5½"

13"

Autumn's Surrender © Margaret Solomon Gunn 2017

Connect Here

Autumn's Surrender © Margaret Solomon Gunn 2017

45°

P

(R is Reverse)

135°

Connect Here

Quilting Motifs
AUTUMN'S SURRENDER

Each quilt inherently possesses its own character, and I believe the quilting for that quilt should reflect that character too. Despite its very rigid and sharp pointed piecing, the tone of AUTUMN'S SURRENDER is softer, emanating a more ethereal message.

Tools Required:
- Air or water eraseable marking pen and chalk marking pencil
- ¼" straight longarm template with ¼" etched lines
- Ronda K. Beyer Double-S longarm template OR combination of 8" and 12" diameter arc longarm templates
- 8", 12", and 20" diameter longarm curved crosshatch templates
- Rope stencil by The Stencil Company.
- ½" straight crosshatched grid stencil OR ruler with ½" markings
- lightbox

Light Blue and Chartreuse Borders

Few quilting motifs carry the grace and movement that this quilt needs better than flowing feathers. The soft blue frame was a perfect place to quilt these because quilting shows better on lighter fabrics. This space is irregular in shape and is made up of several shades of blue silk fabric. The space is more united by quilting one motif throughout all of it, than if it were broken into several sections. Additionally, feathers are easy to tailor to unusual shapes more than almost any other motif.

To get a feather pattern that exactly fits the odd space which could also be symmetrically repeated to the other sides of the quilt, I traced the boundary of the blue border onto tracing paper. The tracing paper enabled an immediate viewing of the motif on the quilt to determine if this was really the best design.

Before quilting anything, the perimeter of the light blue and chartreuse borders should be stabilized with ditch stitching, shown here in pink. Either a clear or coordinating color silk thread will yield the least noticeable ditch stitching. The detail quilting is stitched using threads that match the silks.

The order of stitching for the light blue border is as follows: Begin with ditch stitching, continuing with the spines of the feathers, feathers, and pebble and echo fillers. Finish with the curved crosshatching.

The pattern for the light blue border quilting consists of undulating feathers and two sections of crosshatching. The pattern, which shows the spine, all feathers and leaves, and crosshatching for ⅛ of the symmetrical border should be enlarged to the space. I only use the pattern to premark the spines using a light box. Use the pattern as a reference to freehand quilt the feathers and leaves. The natural undulations and variations in the quilting are beautiful.

Placing hook curls and leaves in approximately the same locations in each section creates the illusion that all sections are identical. As shown below, the only markings (done in water soluble blue pen) besides the spine are a pattern centerline and general locations for the boundaries of feathers.

A variety of curve/circle templates may be used to help make the curves smooth. It is important not to quilt the feathers completely to the edge of each boundary. Pebbles and echo quilting placed around the tips of the feathers provide further definition. The echo quilting helps to pop the feathers, while the feathers create added texture to the background.

Section A is curved crosshatch using a 12" template. The crosshatchings are spaced ¼" apart. Section B is also curved crosshatch, but the 20" arc template is used. This section gets a ¼" frame and then ½" spaced crosshatching. These sections appear harmonious on the quilt because they are both similar, but the variety in the motif provides a pleasing difference. The illustration below shows how to curve crosshatch these sections continuously.

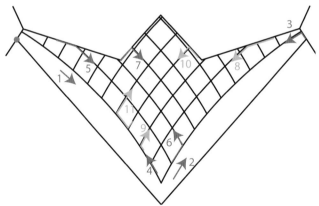

Free flowing feathers were also chosen for the chartreuse border near the center of the quilt. This light colored fabric, like the blue border, was also pieced in an irregular shape. The feathers filled it nicely.

The quilting design for the chartreuse border consists of a feathery design similar to the light blue border as well as a scrolled frame. The addition of this frame accomplishes several things. First, it creates a point of visual interest because it is in contrast to the feathering in the space. It brings cohesion to the overall quilting design because this is a repeated element. A similar scroll frame is placed on the eight chartreuse triangles of an outer border. Lastly, the scroll frame creates a secondary pattern. It may look like a couple of arcing lines on the sketch, but when viewing the entire quilt it is a lovely arching frame. These are all items I strive to achieve in the various items I design into the quilting.

As with other patterns, take care to enlarge the pattern before transferring the pattern to the quilt. Like before, I only mark the scrolls and the spine and allow the feathers to be freehand quilted. The feather motifs in this border were stitched with a chartreuse silk thread. Because the area is smaller than that of the light blue borders, there is no echo quilting or pebbling outside of the feathers.

The scrolled frame is actually stitched in a slightly contrasting light blue silk thread. Using the 12" arc or circle template, first stitch the upper and lower frames for this motif, then quilt the outline of the scrolls. The area around the scroll is densely stitched with lines that follow the contours and curves of the scrolls. In reality, any dense filler will pop this pattern to the positive quilting space, so choose your favorite. The contrasting color thread for this dense fill yields an unexpected and nice alteration to the fabric color.

Brown Octagon

It is a known fact that it is harder to get quilting to show on darker fabrics unless you want to use a starkly contrasting color thread. Light bounces off of patterns and fabrics differently. As a result, I often design simpler geometric quilting motifs for darker fabrics, as the eye can discern simple textures more easily than something more complex. The dark brown octagon falls into this category. Despite designing simpler quilting for the brown, I still chose to break up the space into a few motifs rather than just one.

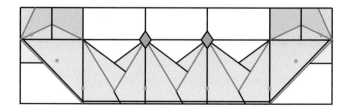

To begin this pattern, outline stitch the perimeter of the brown section. The previous illustration shows the brown fabric modified to yellow and the pattern is rotated 45° for visibility. Pink lines indicate where the quilt should have ditch stitching. The location of the green dots, whose location is eyeballed, should be marked with chalk. These will be used in the next steps. The entire perimeter of the octagon has a row of outline stitching placed ¼" from the outer border of this section. It is simplest to quilt this first before getting into the details.

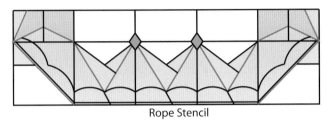
Rope Stencil

Next, a border of scallops is quilted, as shown in the above illustration, by connecting the aforementioned and chalk-marked green dots. The larger scallops, both left and right sides, are quilted with a 12" diameter arc, while the smaller ones in the center are quilted with an 8" diameter arc or circle. When a pieced quilt has strong linear lines, as this one does, I find it pleasing to introduce curves whenever possible to soften the look.

(Commercially purchased at The Stencil Co., quiltingstencils.com)

Beneath the arcs, a rope design was quilted using a commercially purchased ¾" rope stencil. While some quilters quilt the rope design freehanded, I feel the stencil makes it simpler and more uniform. Stencils can bring an added dimension to freehand quilting, as well as an immense variety of different patterns to one's repertoire.

The stencil is marked onto the area indicated, centering it between the arcs and the straight stitching. When turning corners with a stencil pattern, I do my best to fudge it. While some stencils do include a 90° corner, having a 45° corner is unheard of. I suggest a finely sharpened chalk pencil, like the ones Bohin makes, or a sharpened piece of school chalk.

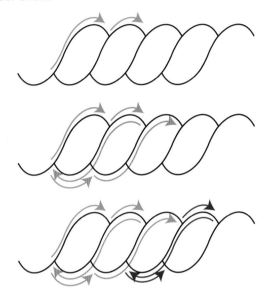

The stitching for the rope is done similarly to the backtracked feather. Stitch one lobe of the rope bottom to top as shown in green. Next, quilt the top of the next lobe. Now, backtrack over the stitching just quilted and quilt the entire lobe shown in pink. Backtrack over the bottom of that lobe and quilt the entire next lobe. This pattern repeats until the entire rope is quilted.

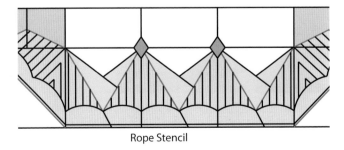
Rope Stencil

Parallel lines are added to the remaining area of the brown octagon. These lines are spaced ½" apart. This illustration shows how these lines are treated at the corners of the pattern. While I do not mark the entire line, I strongly suggest marking the top and bottom locations for each line. I also take care to center the line spacing at the apex of each triangle so that each looks consistent. To enhance the textural appearance of this section, every other space is backfilled with a dense squiggly filler (refer to the Squiggly Line Fill on page 43). You may use whatever dense fill you like best.

Octagon Parts

There are eight sections which I call Octagon Parts located outboard of the brown octagon. They are comprised of a chartreuse triangle and two pale blue diamonds. Four are adjacent to the actual quilt

corners, as shown in the previous photo. The other four at the top, bottom, and sides of the quilt are like the photo below. They are identical except for the quilting outboard of the frame and pebbles.

First, let's look at the parts of these that are the same. Begin by ensuring that the chartreuse triangle and the boundary of the pale blue diamonds are ditch stitched. This motif has several components, each of which contribute something different to the overall quilt.

A curved frame, indicated in green, and a row of ¼" diameter pebbles are quilted inside of the blue diamonds. The line is not marked, but rather quilted using the Double S ruler positioning the ruler from point to point. I love this template because it creates smooth curves with points of inflection, meaning that there is an outer curve that transgresses to an inside curve. The reason this particular curve was selected for AUTUMN'S SURRENDER is simple. The secondary pattern created from all eight sections is a gorgeous curving star shape. Ronda's ruler is approximately 14" x 6" and includes curves from about 8" to 12" diameter.

The string of pearl/pebbles may be quilted one of three different ways and the method chosen is largely the choice of the quilter. The most common is probably the first illustration below, where each circle is outlined one and a half times. Some quilters refer to this as a Figure 8 technique. In areas where inaccurate tracing might show, I often choose either the second or third methods since they do not require any over tracing. Where it is easy to get into a rhythm and freehand the pebbles using the first method, the latter two are often simpler if the pebbles are marked.

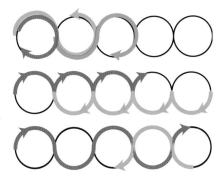

Note that the pale blue silk is quilted with a pale blue silk thread, while the chartreuse triangle is quilted with a wasabi green colored silk thread. I am only interested in generating texture with the quilting, not visible thread.

Restart the quilting thread near the point of the chartreuse triangle. Following the pink quilting, this space is filled with free-flowing feathers. They are the backtracking variety, but do not have to be. Casually use the edge of the pebbles as a spine. Feathers are quilted down the side of the chartreuse triangle. When the end of the triangle is reached, a hook curl is stitched ending back at the spine.

Now, use the side of the hook curl as the spine for the next section of feathers. These feathers flare in the opposite direction. Stop quilting feathers when there is a section of blue remaining just large enough for one last section of feathers or about 1½".

Just as before, use the side of the last feather as the spine for the remaining patch of feathers. Where the last feather would normally be, quilt a leaf instead. Now, backtrack down the spine that has been created, past the starting point, to the location where the feathers begin on the opposite diamond. Repeat the same procedure. Attempt to place the hook curl in the same location, as this will make the feather sprays appear more symmetrical. I usually count the number of feathers, as well as make a visual mark where I should end before quilting the feathers in the opposite direction.

It is important to remember that this is freehand quilting. The natural inflections and variations of how we quilt are beautiful and should not be viewed as mistakes.

For the octagon units like those shown above, the ¼" spaced curved lines located outboard of the frame and pebbles are quilted with the Double S medium ruler. This parallel line quilting is simple, but helps to set off the feather sprays nicely. The octagon units with the filled clamshell pattern will be discussed in the section entitled Corners on page 95.

The natural inflections and variations of how we quilt are beautiful and should not be viewed as mistakes.

Next, let's look at the quilting on the chartreuse triangles. Begin by quilting a row of echo quilting ¼" from the boundary of the two short sides of the triangle. This helps to make the shape of the triangle a little more visible.

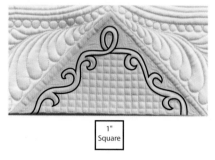

The detail quilting on the chartreuse triangles requires some premarking. First, ensure that the pattern is enlarged until the square measures accurately 1" square. The scroll pattern should be premarked on the quilt using a lightbox and a fine tip water soluble marking pen. The spacing between the lines of the scroll motif is only about ¼" so if the design is to be seen after quilting, it is important that it is carefully marked. Fatter tip pens do not trace smaller scale designs such as this as accurately.

Very carefully quilt the scroll. It has to be freehanded so if you need a little more machine control consider using the micro-handles and/or placing two to three yards of folded fabric behind the head of the machine shown below. This added weight creates additional drag, thereby increasing controllability. Densely quilt with either lines or stipple outboard of the scroll motif to increase its visibility.

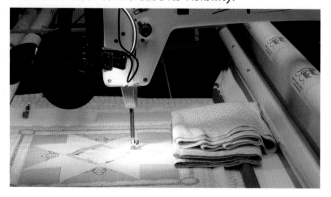

The last thing to quilt on the chartreuse triangles is the ¼" straight crosshatch. Though this quilt has several types of crosshatching of differing sizes, the fact that the crosshatching repeats in different locations only adds to the cohesiveness of the quilting. Consider this when designing quilting for your own quilts.

Gold Star Points

Gold star points are located in four places. Each star is made up of three diamondlike units.

Ditching noted in blue, echo quilting noted in red

Begin by ditch stitching (SID) the periphery of the gold diamonds, as shown above in blue. Since this SID involves quilting on both a pale and a dark fabric, it would be best to stitch the ditching in a clear thread. Next, using a gold silk thread, a row of echo quilting is stitched ¼" from the edge of the diamonds as shown above in red. This line of quilting highlights the diamond shape.

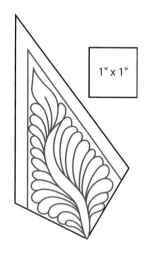

The quilting of the feathers in the diamonds may be accomplished one of two ways. Prior to quilting, use the pattern given above, enlarged as indicated, and mark the spine and feathers onto the quilt top using a light box. The alternative is to make a cardstock template of only the curving spine from the enlarged template. While the quilt is loaded on the longarm quilting machine, trace the cardstock pattern of the spine and freehand quilt the feathers. I did the second option on AUTUMN'S SURRENDER, as I do not feel it is necessary to exactly replicate each diamond. Remember, freehand variations are beautiful and natural. Please feel free to quilt these in a way that is most comfortable to you.

Corners

The quilting designed for the corners of AUTUMN'S SURRENDER is both complex and intertwined. It brings motifs from other areas of the pieced quilt into the quilting, creating a more cohesive design. The diamond shape from the appliqué repeats at the corners of the green border. Rows of pearls or pebbles are repeated here as well. Because this border is fairly complicated, several components should be premarked prior to loading the quilt or sandwiching it for quilting.

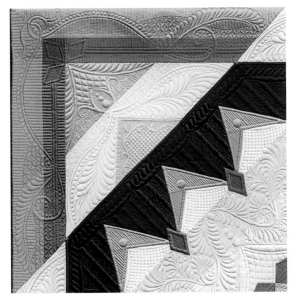

The design of the corners was sketched onto tracing paper for easy visualization at actual scale. The pattern is on page 97. After enlarging the pattern

to the appropriate size, premark key design motifs including the diamonds, scrolls, ½" grid, and straight lines in the 2" border using a lightbox. Many of these items intertwine each other and are difficult to align without premarking.

First ditch stitch the inner side of the 2" green border. This stabilizes the corner and ensures that the line of the border will remain straight. Next, baste the outer edge of the 2" green border indicated by the green dashed line. Again, we want this border to appear straight. It cannot be completely ditch stitched since other components like scrolls and feathers are quilted through it, but the basting will hold the correct positioning. Remove this basting before any of the dense fillers are quilted. Now, quilt the detail motifs located outboard of the chartreuse triangle indicated in pink lines. The long sweeping curves are quilted with either the 12" or 20" diameter arcs, while other shapes are freehanded.

After quilting the scroll frames and feather spine that are in the outermost border, follow with the ¼" string of pearls (pebbles) and freehanded feathers indicated in blue. Now, move back to the 2" green inner border and quilt the diamonds and straight lines that run parallel to the border. Areas marked A, B, and C have a premarked grid and will receive a grid-based filler shortly.

Quilt the space above the diamonds with ½" curved crosshatching using the 20" arc template denoted in yellow. Other indicated areas receive a ¼" spaced parallel line filler. For the greatest effect, take care to align the lines when they are broken by an obstruction. Now all that remains are the dense grid-based fills.

Quilting of the background space beneath the octagon parts marked A relies on having a ½" grid. I believe it is easier to premark this grid using a commercially purchased ½" stencil grid, but it is also possible to mark it as the quilt is being quilted using a template. This space will be quilted with a filled clamshell design.

Grid-based fillers, especially those adapted from Japanese Sashiko patterns, are really lovely. They finish extremely flat and do an excellent job of showing off the positive relief of any quilting around them. Because they are very dense patterns, it is best that they are quilted with thin threads. This is quilted with silk 100 wt. thread. When the filled clamshell pattern is finished, it will look like the photo below.

1" square

Now, let's step through how you get from a marked grid to the pattern on page 96.

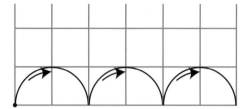

Find a convenient place to start quilting. The clamshell pattern is nothing more than quilting a quarter circle in every grid cell. I think of it as continuously bumping semicircles across the grid, until the end is reached. If there is an obstruction, it may be easier to mark where the semicircle should end on the obstruction with a marking pen.

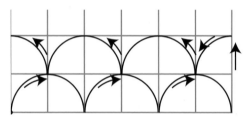

Every other row of the bumps is offset by one grid cell to achieve the clamshell shape.

The entire space should be filled prior to adding the dense details.

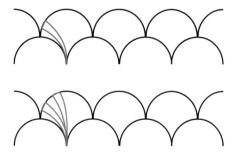

To create the clamshell fill, begin at the point of the clamshell. Think of the filler as consisting of several fans quilted within each clamshell. Because a fine thread is being used, it is easy to traverse or backtrack across the arc of the clamshell when making these fans and not have it show.

After filling the clamshell with four or five fans, carefully trace to the next clamshell and begin filling it in the same fashion. While it is easy to fill these randomly, I find it more orderly to fill directly across in rows. You will find your own rhythm.

The areas marked B and C are quilted with pumpkin seed fill, which is also seen on Japanese sashiko patterns. This pattern is sometimes referred to in the quilting community as continuous curves or orange peel. This time the pattern is being quilted using an on-point grid. Like the clamshells, I densely filled the background of the pattern.

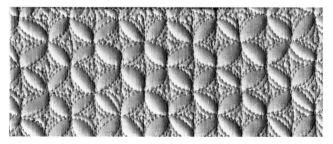

There are several options for how to mark this grid, but I suggest that the grids are marked prior to loading the quilt and on a firm table. First, you can use the same ½" grid that was used for the clamshells, just orient the template 45° from vertical. Secondly, these templates may be purchased with the grid already in the on-point orientation. This is probably the simplest method, and it is what I did. As a last resort, the grid can be marked on angle using a rotary cutting grid-style template.

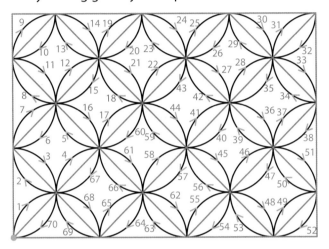

The first step is to quilt the basic pumpkin seed pattern. Start at the green dot and follow the numbers. This pattern can be stitched continuously in a number of different ways.

After the outline of the pattern is completed, it will resemble the unfilled pumpkin seed photo. For those that prefer less dense quilting, you can stop now. To fill the pattern, simply choose your favorite filler, set the stitches per inch to about 16-18, and fill the diamond shapes of the pattern. I have done this pattern using a stipple as well as by stitching arcs that run parallel to the melon shapes. Both look equally as good.

Center Star Block

This photo shows the frames and basic motifs of the center Star block. The ¼" wide frame indicated in pink was premarked so that it appears interlocking. To do this, simply mark the location of the blue dots by eyeballing these in the approximate center of the space. Mark the curved frame with a 20" arc or circle template. If you do not care for the interlocking look, try quilting point to point without premarking. Begin by ditch stitching the pieced and appliquéd elements. Quilt the pink frames followed by the feathers shown in green, and the details on the center star.

At this point, two areas remain. The large arching spaces are ¼" curve crosshatched using the 20" template, while all of the other spaces receive a very tight stipple. The stippling makes the interlocking frame more visible. Take care to use a very short stitch length about 18–20 stitches per inch on the stipple and double check that your machine tension is optimum. There is no taking out stippling this dense!

½" Double-Fold Binding

Cut 3⅜" wide strips from the length of fabric from interfaced Silk Radience, 245" total.

Using Zen Garden binding instructions make double-fold binding.

Beaded decoration was added between the quilt and the binding.

BOUQUET ROYALE

80" x 80"

Inspiration, Design Process, and Finishing

In the summer of 2013, I quilted a client quilt. Her quilt consisted of 25 bold print elongated Hexagon blocks, each finishing at 12" square and placed in a straight setting with white sashing and borders. She chose bright Kaffe Fassett fabrics mixed with batiks. The quilt was a replica of the Lucy Boston pattern first introduced around 1950, and I was intrigued with the interlocking appearance of the block.

I had been doing an increasing amount of hand appliqué. With my business keeping me busy during the day, time for making my own quilts was limited. The idea of having a hand piecing project that I could stitch upstairs in the evenings rather than in my basement studio was pleasing.

Using my math background and EQ7, I drafted the elongated Hexagon block, but created my pattern for a smaller 8¼" block. My method for the Hexagon blocks allowed for hand piecing rather than English paper piecing. In October of 2013, I set out with a brightly colored stack of large scale prints taken from my stash to make a test block.

My learnings from this initial block were many. The blocks were time consuming, taking nearly five hours to make just one from fabric selection to pressing. It was all too easy to underestimate how many yards of large scale print was needed in order to get eight identical pieces. Though it went completely against my grain, I had to accept that there would be large amounts of waste to make these blocks.

The blocks were simple to piece and my stitching method and jig worked successfully. Most importantly, the kaleidoscoping effect of the fabrics looked phenomenal. I just needed to buy another 8-10 yards of large scale florals from which to create fabric Swiss cheese!

Sometimes, when I am making a quilt, I begin with a complete plan and pattern. This quilt was different. I decided I'd make a bunch of the Hexagon blocks and see where they led me. Each of the blocks I made was different from the last. I did not have a clear direction of how large the quilt might be, or how it would be best to arrange the blocks. Actual blocks were needed before I could design a layout and select additional fabrics for the quilt.

Somewhere in the block making process, I decided that they'd look interesting set in champagne-colored silk. In my mind, it was a bit risky mixing cottons with silk, but the floral Hexagon blocks looked incredible when placed on the silk as a background. The champagne color and the sheen of the silk was rich and luscious. Silk quilts like no other fabric and I knew it would make this quilt memorable. The outer round of squares and triangles on the blocks were pieced in the silk. How the remainder of the quilt would evolve was still anybody's guess.

The 25 blocks took about six months to make. As I was nearing completion of these, I began designing the remainder of the quilt. I knew the background would be in part green, since this color makes me happy and was a common color in many blocks.

The other thing I discovered was that my 25 blocks could be arranged in a way to create a definite medallion center and it would feature my favorites of all the blocks, the orange and coral ones. I am a total sucker for orange, especially when it comes to flowers. These just remind me of my garden.

Using EQ7 to develop a layout for this quilt was challenging on account of the many curved sections. It was probably possible, but beyond my skills with the program! I had made a hand drawn sketch, but I like to have an electronic version as it is a tool to test different fabric colors. The version I created with EQ7 lacks some realism, but it served the purpose. My hand sketch would be the basis for the design and patterns would be enlarged from this 8½" x 11" sketch.

I added an unusually wide 10" - 11" outer border, partly to help ground the busyness of the colorful blocks and partly to hold some pretty appliqué. Color By Hand, out of Newport, Kentucky, custom dyed four pieces of silk Radiance in shades of green that coordinated with the greens in the prints. These silks would make up a set of duo-tone ribbons that would intertwine on the border. My last touch was the addition of the deep coral shoestring bows. These were added as an attempt to draw the deeper orange and coral shades of the center medallion outward.

Hand stitching the ribbon appliqué was time consuming, so I was busy designing the quilting for Bouquet Royale before the quilt top was remotely close to finished.

I began designing the quilting for the massive green outer border first. Goals for this border included making it feel regal, creating a unique and geometric style of quilting here, and allowing the quilting to play peek-a-boo behind the appliqué. I borrowed part of a design I used on my SPRINGITME IN THE GEISHA"S GARDEN quilt that I finished in 2014. The ¾" silk dots appliquéd along the border were again added for a textural effect. The deep green silk, a perfect match to the outer border fabric, was used for the centers of the flowers I was going to quilt. The variation in sheen helped to give the motifs of this large border definition. The flowers, which conveniently tied into the garden theme of the quilt, were also used to anchor the Cathedral Windows which I was planning for the border.

The outer border is a deeply colored fabric. To keep the border from appearing too busy, I planned a design that was geometric, well framed, and relatively simple to stitch monochromatically with a dark green thread. A scale model was drawn, and revisions were substantially made.

I also planned to connect the flowers with a ribbon motif, thereby bringing an aspect of the appliqué into the quilting. Much to my frustration, when I went to quilt the first of these large green borders, I accidentally stitched the crosshatching in the wrong

space! The design was modified once again, this time on the fly rather than unstitching.

While I viewed the massive green border and the champagne silk as harder areas to design on account of their high visibility, the colorful and heavily printed octagon squares were nearly as challenging. I planned to stitch using a heavier thread because it would balance the prints nicely. I also planned for

sections of more geometric quilting. Crosshatching and line work typically show better on prints than nondescriptive fillers.

The initial design placed a floral motif at the center of the block. My chosen design would mostly ignore the hexagon piecing lines of the block, only using intersections as guidelines. Unsure how the pebbles would show for the final version of the design, sets of parallel lines were used instead, with some dense filling to better accentuate the lines.

As it turns out, the final design was slightly different yet, as feathers were stitched around the outer area of the block. I loved how the ¼" curved crosshatching gave the illusion of each flower having a little spider web.

The blank squares and setting triangles of the hexagon corners needed to be designed beforehand since this is an open and showy location. I began by drafting a design on paper for these spaces, including a swirling border adapted from a small commercial template.

This design was different for me, a characteristic I strive to give each successive quilt. Because it didn't read as "garden" or "regal," attributes I was trying to convey with my quilting, I went back to the drawing board. The next idea actually led to the design I did use. It consisted of a floral scroll border with leaves, flowers, and feathers. The inner frame

copied the scalloped motif, a shape already prevalent in the appliqué. At the very center, I used a small diamond of a basket weave pattern (stencil by Emily Senuta).

Before quilting, I feel it is important to audition how the many individual designs work together. Scanned images for the quilting motifs I planned to use for sections of the setting corners were overlaid onto a digital photo of the corner using Photoshop. Being able to visualize designs before stitching increases the odds that a design won't get unstitched later. It shows small areas that may need tweaking and helps to give ideas for what fillers may look best for the remaining open areas. In this case, it also enabled me to see the potential effectiveness of the frame placed at the curving green border, an idea which not so oddly came to me in the middle of one sleepless night.

Quilting designs for the center medallion were not nailed down until 75% of the quilt was actually stitched. This space was not just left open. Rather, the nine blocks were quilted and basting was placed to keep the unit from shifting. I talk a lot about the center focal of the quilt and I had yet to create this for Bouquet Royale. I knew I needed more than nine identically quilted blocks to draw in the viewer. I also knew that

some of the motifs I created for other areas of the quilt needed to be repeated in the center medallion too. Repetition creates cohesion (repeat with me…). With these goals in mind, the design progressed.

A scalloped frame copied from the four nosegay appliqués was placed around every other block. I used the pale green setting squares to hold feature

diamonds with fanned lines, helping to frame the center block at a higher visibility creating an interesting optical illusion with quilting.

A small portion of the floral scroll feather design from the hexagon corners was repeated on the center medallion. It was subtle, but seemed appropriate. Similarly, I also used the basket weave stencil design in a few locations.

Designs for the scalloped border of the medallion were also auditioned and after sketching at actual size, a winner was chosen.

Only one feature of the design was lacking, a dense fill to connect all of the unquilted background areas of the silk. Resisting the easy approach of just stitching a dense stipple, I searched for something different, something more unique. My instinct was that a linear treatment would show the delineation between the other stitched motifs more effectively than something like pebbling or another tiny stippled shape. I was looking for a design that was more than just tight lines. I wanted it to be a pattern in and of itself. The chosen design of ⅛" spaced lines was challenging to execute with good accuracy and the sheen of the silk showed every time the spacing was not perfect. It also exemplifies when there is not a perfect 90° angle on a block.

For a while, I seriously considered removing every bit of this filler; though beautiful and perfect, it was just not quite appropriate for this slightly imperfect quilt. I think all quilters hit this point on a quilt, the point when we are over 500 hours into a project and just want to be done. It is all too easy to second guess our skills and choices. I know it happens, and I can often predict when it will happen. The truth is, I loved this quilt and it needed to be finished. I loved this filler, as it gave the silk the appearance of a rich, old fashioned embossed tin ceiling. I pushed on.

It is no secret that once the quilting is finished, there is still a significant chunk of time left for adding things like binding, embroidery, and other minute finishing touches. To say that the devil is in the details is an understatement! I like my quilts to have as much of a finished, polished look as possible. Sometimes decisions to add details are simply for the sake of adding the detail, such as the piping at the binding, but other times the decision is borne out of a need to cover something else up!

When I finished the linear fill work, I was irritated by how the ⅛" lines did not always come into these intersections squarely. Many times they approached creating a rectangle of lines that highlighted small inaccuracies. My solution to appliqué tiny champagne silk buttonlike dots, in hindsight, was brilliant. It covered up the offending area and added a beautiful finishing touch very much in keeping with the style of the quilt.

Most finishing details are not really cover-ups. I went back after the longarm quilting was completed and using my Janome® machine and a 30 wt. Tire silk thread, added some heavier accent stitching. The heavier thread matches the sheen of the quilting, but gives an added emphasis to the area outlined. There are also areas where a deep green #5 perle cotton embroidery floss is appliquéd with a fine matching silk thread to create a finished edge.

I absolutely love this quilt. I love the colors, the fabrics, and the fact that I was able to apply my design aesthetic and create something beautiful. Recreating old, traditional patchwork patterns using a more modern and unexpected mix of bold prints and satiny silk makes this quilt different and memorable. I know each and every one of the trials, tribulations, and issues encountered during its creation and construction. It is not perfect, but it is rewarding to have judges recognize it for the creativity and workmanship. That is why I do this business. Sharing what I love with others makes all of the many hours worthwhile.

Awards

World of Beauty Award, IQF Houston, 2016
Masterpiece Quilt, NQA, 2015
Best of Show, HMQS, 2015
Best of Show, AQS Chattanooga, 2015
Solitaire Award, MQS, 2016
Best Machine Quilting, Mancuso Mid-Atlantic, 2017
Best Longarm Workmanship, AQS Daytona, 2016
Best Longarm Workmanship, AQS Lancaster, 2016
Best Longarm Workmanship, AQS Des Moines, 2015
Best Machine Quilting, MQX East, 2015
1st Place, Shipshewana Quilt Festival, 2016
1st Place, MQX East, 2015
2nd Place, Road to California, 2016
2nd Place, NQA, 2015
3rd Place, AQS Syracuse, 2016

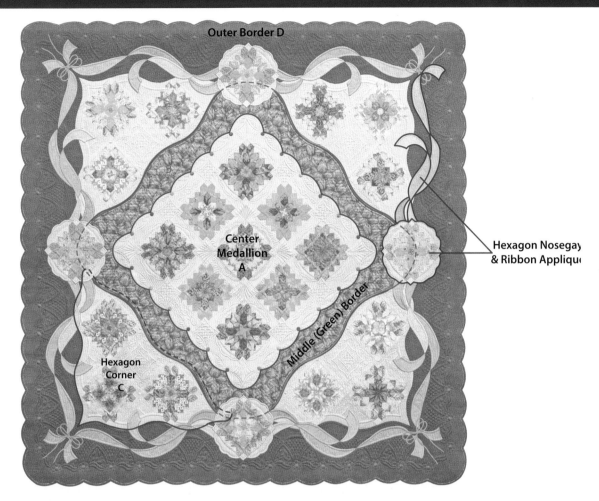

Fabric Requirements

Color	Yardage	Location
Dark green – cotton	5¼	Outer border, binding
Green monotone print – cotton	2⅛	Middle Border *If you want this for binding piping get an additional ⅔ yard
C – Kiwi green silk	⅜	Smaller appliqué ribbons, central medallion
D – Dark kiwi green silk	⅜	Smaller appliqué ribbons
A – Sage green silk	½	Longer appliqué ribbons
B – Dark sage green silk	½	Longer appliqué ribbons
Dark green silk – uninterfaced	½	Bias trim (uninterfaced), 60 appliqué circles
Coral batik	FQ	Bow appliqué
Champagne silk	3¾	Multiple places
Assorted purples (cottons, batiks)	Several small scraps	36 appliqué circles on the outer medallion
Interfacing – Pellon Bi-Stretch Light	11	
6-8 Large scale prints	1½ – 1¾ each	For fussy cutting Hexagon blocks

Cutting Chart for Champagne Silk

Cutting Chart for Champagne Silk

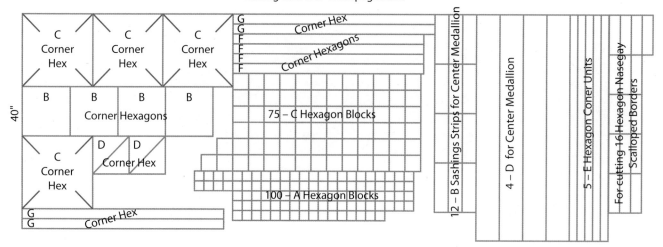

Cutting Diagram for Dark Green

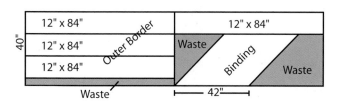

Note about Wasted Fabric

The way the pieces for BOUQUET ROYALE are cut yields a good amount of waste. I like to think of it as scrap stash. It is hard to fussy cut without having waste. The middle green border is also made in a way that optimizes its construction, rather than minimizing its required fabric. It is recommended that the outer green border be cut along the length of the fabric rather than cross grain, which requires more fabric. It also yields a less stretchy, more stable edge. As a quilter, you might make different choices to reduce fabric amounts, but I strive to design and make quilts that optimize ease of construction and flatness. A technically well-made quilt will cause fewer issues to make.

Elongated Hexagon Block

Each Hexagon block requires 24 hexagons, 12 triangles, and 4 squares. The triangles and squares are

cut from interfaced silk Radiance. The hexagons are fussy cut from four different prints. You may choose other fabrics if fussy cutting is not your preference.

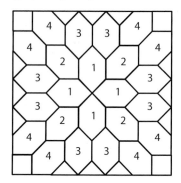

Each block requires:
4 hexagons of print 1
4 hexagons of print 2
8 hexagons of print 3
8 hexagons of print 4

Two tools should be created for more easily cutting these pieces. First, a plastic template of the exact finished elongated hexagon is traced from Template B. The hand stitching lines are drawn onto over 500 hexagons with this template so it should be made from a material whose shape will not change or deform. Template plastic is ideal.

Secondly, a fabric cutting jig should be created. Cardboard or cardstock (or even an old cereal box!) works fine. Trace the plastic hexagon onto a 2¾"

square of cardstock. Using a ruler, add an exact ¼" allowance along all six sides of the hexagon. Carefully cut along the outer lines, leaving a hexagon-shaped hole in the jig. This peek-a-boo template is placed over the print patterns on the fabric to align the placement so multiple identical patches may be cut. Using the reverse of this jig obscures the pattern of the fabric that needs to be seen.

Finished size 8¼" x 8¼". Make 25.

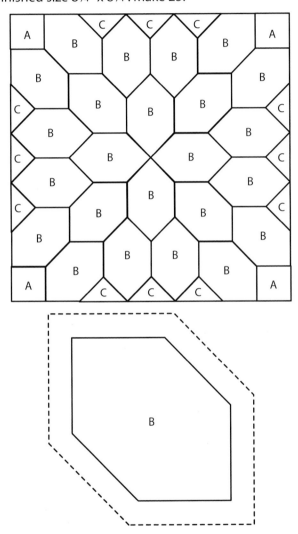

Rotary Cutting

For each block cut (3) 2⅞" x 2⅞" squares from interfaced champagne silk. Cut into 4 triangles along the diagonals.

For the whole quilt, cut 75 squares.

For each block cut (4) 1¾" x 1¾" squares from interfaced champagne silk.

For the whole quilt, cut 100 squares.

Pieces A and C are slightly oversized so the entire block can be cleanly trimmed to 8¾" x 8¾" once pieced.

Templates

Cut B from prints.

Obtaining a desirable Hexagon block is a surreptitious happening. I find that if I cut sets of either 4 or 8 identical hexagons and mix and match them, appealing blocks will result. If a particular set of hexagons is cut and does not look just right for a certain block, it will probably look good on another block. Play with them and be patient with this part of the process. The hexagon pieces shown here are leftovers to show the process of creating the Hexagon block.

A piece of 100 grit sandpaper is sandwiched between a firm surface and the cotton fabric to prevent shifting. With a sharp pencil, trace the smaller hexie template on the backside of the fabric. This marks the stitch line. Center the cardboard jig over this, and trace to create cutting lines.

You will need a 40 or 50 wt. cotton thread in several coordinating colors to change color when the colors of your fabrics change. Cotton threads have more grip than finer threads, so they hold the hand stitching securely. Knots are less prone to pulling open.

Looking at the seams of my hand pieced blocks I notice they look as secure as anything I machine stitch. As for a hand piecing needle, I find that a hand appliqué needle works great. Be sure to choose one that is not too short.

Many quilters would choose to piece these blocks using traditional English Paper Piecing (EPP) techniques. I devised the method described next to do two things: eliminate the need for basting fabric around paper and to create a block that allows the seams to not all be pressed open.

Starting at the center of the block, lay out two of the Print 1 hexagons.

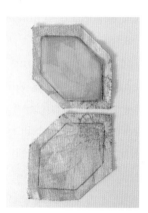

Place them right sides together, placing a pin through the corners of each hexagon to achieve perfect alignment.

When aligned, place 2-3 pins to secure the seam, and then remove the alignment pins in the corners.

Each seam is stitched individually. Tie a knot in the end of the thread and start the seam a couple stitches from the end of the marked seam. This is equivalent to backstitching with the sewing machine. When the corner is reached, reverse direction and use tiny running stitches. Stitch the length of the seam, turn around, stitch 2-3 more stitches, and finish the seam with a knot. Take approximately 10-11 stitches per inch.

Do not stitch beyond the marked seam line so you can control the direction the seam allowances will press when the entire block is stitched.

Repeat steps 1-2 for the other two Print 1 hexagons.

Set the two Print 1 units to be stitched together, seaming the two seams as described and individually. This is the center of the block.

It should look like this.

Finger press the center unit and lay out the Print 2 hexagons. Always lay out the hexagons so the orientation of the pattern or print is consistent.

Add the Print 2 hexagons by stitching inset or Y seams. Sew the seams one at a time to simplify the process. Stick a pin through each corner at either end of the seam to align the two blocks.

One of the alignment pins goes into the center seam. Once aligned, place 2-3 pins to hold the seam and stitch using the method described.

Gently pull the corner with the white dot over to the other location on the piecing with a white dot.

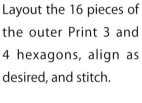

Align and pin. When stitching, take care to keep the seam smooth. The finished inset seam should look like this.

Repeat steps 6 and 7 for the remaining three Print 2 hexagons.

The backside of this block appears a little bit messy, but is just fine.

It will press perfectly when the block is finished.

Layout the 16 pieces of the outer Print 3 and 4 hexagons, align as desired, and stitch.

Using a ruler and a water or air erasable marking pen, indicate the ¼" seam allowance on the back of the squares and triangles.

It is important that these markings are removed prior to pressing the finished block so that they are not heat set into the block permanently.

Trim the blocks to 8¾" square.

Hand stitch the squares and triangles onto the Hexagon block.

Carefully press the block from the backside, taking care to press each seam to one side or the other rather than open to help facilitate stitching in the ditch when quilting. Use a little starch during pressing to help to keep the bias edges of the block in shape. Any starch sprayed onto the silk Radiance will appear to dull its sheen. Washing or blocking the finished quilt will remove the starch and the sheen will return to its original luster.

The finished, pressed, and trimmed block is stunning from both the front and the back.

Center Medallion A

Assembly Diagram

A – (9) 8¾" x 8¾" Hexagon blocks (trimmed size)

B – (12) 2½" x 8¾" champagne sashing

C – (4) 2½" x 2½" kiwi green silk C squares

D – (4) 5¼" x 40" champagne silk borders

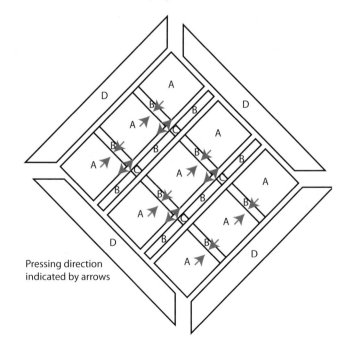

Pressing direction indicated by arrows

Construct the center medallion row by row.

Rows with Hexagon blocks should have the seams pressed toward the sashing.

Rows of sashing and stones should have the seams pressed toward the sashing.

Assemble the three rows of Hexagon blocks and two rows of sashing, pressing all the seams toward the sashing.

The outer border pieces are cut as rectangles and will be mitered at the corners and get the edge scalloped later.

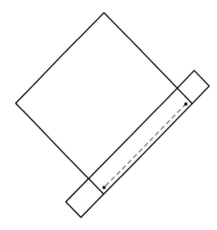

Center one D border on the center square. The border is longer.

Stitch the first border onto the center square starting and stopping stitching ¼" from the edge of the square using back stitches.

Press seams toward the border.

Attach the D border strip to the side opposite this border next.

Press the seams outwards.

Adding Borders 3 & 4

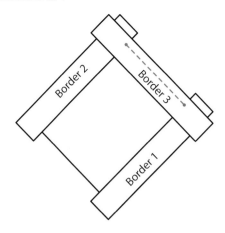

Lay the Border 3 piece over the edge.

Stitch from where the hexagon center meets Borders 1 and 2, back stitching to secure the seam.

Press seams toward the border.

Attach Border 4 the same way as Border 3 and press the seams outward.

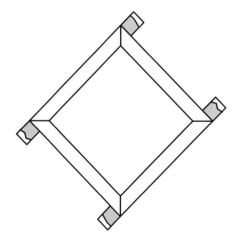

To miter the corners, fold the ends of Borders 3 and 4 so the ends align with Borders 1 and 2.

Using a square rotary cutting guide with a 45° line indicated, fine tune the alignment of the miter to ensure the corner is square.

Press the corner.

Set the corner with pins and hand stitch the miter or lightly glue baste with clear glue, heat set, and machine stitch on the backside along the crease.

Trim the excess from the miter seam to ¼" and press the miter seam open.

The center medallion should now be 38¾" x 38¾" measuring edge to edge.

Mark (do not cut) the scalloped edge using the Curved Template #1 placing one side at the border centerline and the other side at the miter of the corner. Use a blue water soluble pen to mark the champagne silk scallops.

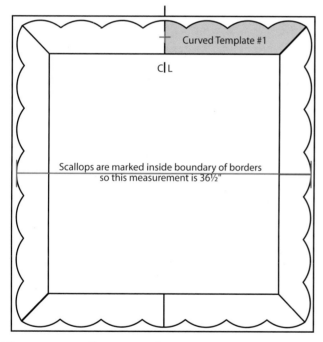

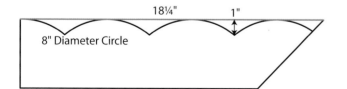

There are 7 scallops per side.

Curved Template #1

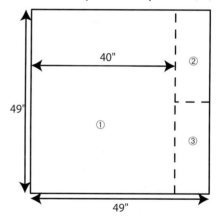

Full size template on pages 127–128.

When the Middle Green Border is cut, it will be reverse appliquéd to this scallop line of the center medallion.

Note: I used reverse appliqué for two reasons. First, it creates a seam under the darker green fabric so there is no chance of the green shadowing through beneath the ivory silk. Second, it is much easier to make clean inside points on the scallop appliqué.

Middle Green Border
Cutting and Prep
Piece 1:
Cut (1) 49" x 40" rectangle from the full width of the fabric.

Pieces 2 and 3:
Cut (2) 9½" x 24¾" rectangles.

Create a 49" x 49" square from pieces 1, 2, and 3.

Press the seams open.

Fold the border in half both ways and along the diagonals. Mark the centerlines of the four sides, the diagonals, and the middle. This is so the center medallion is appliquéd in exactly the proper place.

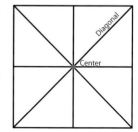

Attaching the Center Medallion to the Middle Border

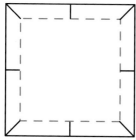

Place the middle border with the right side up on top of the center medallion, which is also right side up.

These two pieces need to be centered with each other using the centerline and diagonal guidelines that are marked.

Gently unfold the middle border to expose the location of the center medallion and adjust as needed. It may be helpful to tape the center medallion to a hard floor and only adjust the middle border.

When ideal placement is achieved, pin the two together very generously.

Turn the pinned pieces over revealing the backsides of both units.

Machine baste using a long stitch on the marked scalloped line. If the marked scallop line does not show through, mark it on the backside.

Baste – –
Clip Middle Border ——

Turn the unit over to the middle border side.

Snip the middle border ¼" to ⅜" inside of the basting.

Reverse hand appliqué the middle border onto the center medallion. Remove a few inches of basting at a time, turn under the seam allowance of the middle border, and hand stitch using a fine matching green thread.

When the middle border is fully reverse appliquéd to the center medallion, trim away the excess silk of the center medallion's D border revealing about ¼" to ⅜" seam allowance.

Remove the air or water soluble pen markings before pressing.

Hexagon Corner C
Make 4

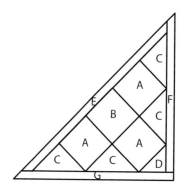

All pieces except A are cut from the interfaced champagne silk.

A – (12) Hexagon blocks finishing 8¼" x 8¼" (measures 8¾" x 8¾" unfinished).

B – Cut (4) 8¾" x 8¾" squares.

C – Cut (4) 12⅞" x 12⅞" squares. Cut in half diagonally both directions.

D – Cut (2) 6¹¹⁄₁₆" x 6¹¹⁄₁₆" squares. Cut in half diagonally.

E – Cut (4) 2½" x 48" rectangles. You can seam this piece at the centerline if need be since this seam will not show. Trim the ends to size after stitching onto the blocks.

F – Cut (4) 1¾" x 35" rectangles. These are oversized on length.

G – Cut (4) 1¾" x 37" rectangles. These are oversized on length.

Note: Although a good portion of pieces E, F, and G will be covered up by the middle border and the outer border, having this material initially present aids in attaining proper alignment of the corners.

Order of Stitching

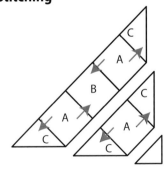

Press in the direction of the arrows.

Stitch the rows together.

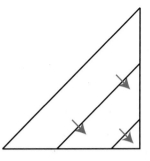

Attach E, press outward.

Attach F, press outward.

Attach G, press outward.

Assembling Hexagon Corners to Quilt

Full size templates are on pages 129–131.

Using Curved Pattern #2, mark the serpentine edge for the middle green border. The pattern should lie neatly at the scallops of the center medallion.

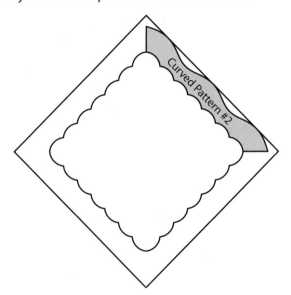

Mark the curved edge on all four sides, then cut the curve.

The exact placement of the four hexagon corners was made on the hardwood floor of my foyer. This process requires a space of at least 8' x 8' and the parallel lines of the wood flooring aided my task in obtaining a square layout. A tile or linoleum floor would also work, though carpet would be more challenging. A large table works well.

Useful Tools:

Measuring tape

Laser level (one laser) or

Laser level square (two lasers 90° apart)

12" square rotary cutting guide

Place the four corners and center on the floor with the center overlapping the corner pieces, as shown on the above diagram. Ensure that the center is straight in its on-point orientation and place something on it to hold it in position (like small bean bags or pattern weights.)

After visual alignment is done, shine a laser from one corner block through two adjacent corner sections to the opposite corner block illustrated above in orange.

Adjust as needed. Move the laser level 90° and repeat.

If you have a laser level square that emits two lasers at 90° to one another, this process can be faster. I did it with a single laser. When aligning these corners, pay particular attention to the location where the middle green border curve crosses the corners of the hexagon corner as shown in the photo below.

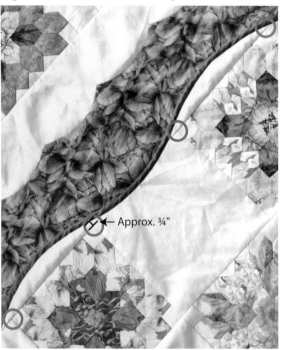

Try to maintain a distance of ¾" between the curved edge of the center and the corners of the Hexagon blocks. As one final check, shine the laser down each diagonal. It should pass through the corners and the center block.

The next photo shows the corners before the F and G silk strips were added, and prior to appliquéing the center medallion and middle border.

When you are satisfied with the placement, pin every inch or so along the curved raw edge of the Middle green border. On a sewing machine, stitch about ⅛" from the edge of the curve using a regular length stitch. This seam and the raw edge will soon be covered with a ⁷⁄₁₆" bias trim made from dark green un-interfaced silk Radiance.

Using the instructions included for making bias stems, make four pieces 50" long. A ⁷⁄₁₆" finished turned edge bias trim requires strips cut 1⅜" wide, or 1" if a conventional bias maker is used.

Center the bias trim over the seam along the exposed edge and appliqué using your favorite appliqué technique, either hand or machine.

Hexagon Nosegays

Four of the Hexagon blocks are made into hexagon nosegays. These are the flower blocks located at the centerline of each of the borders from which the appliqué ribbons emerge. After being prepared with a turned edge, they are appliquéd to the quilt by hand or machine.

Each of these 4 units requires 1 Hexagon block and 4 Nosegay Scalloped borders made from interfaced champagne silk.

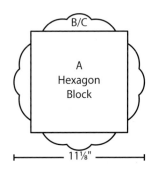

Guidelines for Creating the Nosegay Scalloped Borders

The Nosegay Scalloped border can be completed using Templar or freezer paper techniques. Pick one template depending on the preferred appliqué method.

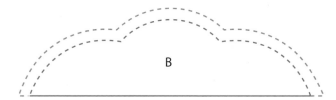

Use template B to prepare appliqués using Templar. Full size template on page 137.

The pink dashed line indicates the template cut line, the orange dashed line indicates fabric cut line.

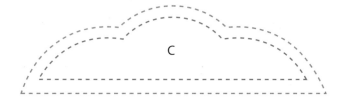

Use template C to appliqué using freezer paper. Full size template on page 137.

The pink dashed line indicates the freezer paper cut line, and the orange dashed line indicates the fabric cut line.

Using Templar

Cut a Templar template using the template marked B. It can be reused. This piece is symmetrical so it is not necessary to reverse the Templar template. The bottom edge of the Templar should be placed exactly at the bottom of a straight cut piece of interfaced silk.

A ¼" seam allowance has already been added to the straight edge of the Templar pattern. Trace ¼" outside of the scalloped edge and cut out the appliqué patch.

The diagonal lines on the photo indicate where the fabric needs to be snipped in order to create a smooth inner point. Clip in toward the point to approximately ¹⁄₁₆" from the template.

Refer to the Preparing Turned Edge Appliqué instructions. Begin pressing the prepared edges with the two inner points and then gently set the scallops. Take your time and smooth the curve as you go.

If the seam allowance is cut too small, the Templar method is harder when using the interfaced silk. Trim the seam to 3/16" after it is starched under to remove excess bulk.

From the front side, the nosegay scallop border is smooth and ready to attach to the Hexagon block.

Using Freezer Paper

Press two pieces of freezer paper together onto each other, leaving the bottom surface waxy. Trace the pattern marked C onto freezer paper for each of the 16 pieces and cut out the patterns. For the interfaced silk, it is easier to prepare freezer paper turned edge appliqué when two layers of freezer-paper are used because it makes a stiffer template. Press these patterns onto the backside of the interfaced silk, leaving adequate room between pieces for seam allowances.

Using a rotary cutting guide, cut an exact ¼" seam allowance along the straight edge of the pattern. The freezer paper pattern does not include any seam allowances. The freezer paper will remain attached to the appliqué patch until it is completely appliquéd onto the quilt.

Cut out each pattern, leaving ¼" outside of the scalloped edge of the pattern. Carefully snip the inside points to within 1/16" of the freezer paper.

Follow the Preparing Turned Edge Appliqué instructions for preparing the edge of the freezer paper appliqué only turning the scalloped edge under.

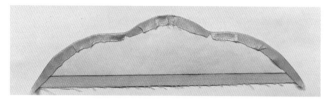

Attaching Nosegay Scalloped Borders to Hexagon Blocks

To attach the nosegay scalloped borders, place the right sides together centering a scalloped border along the edge of a Hexagon block, and pin.

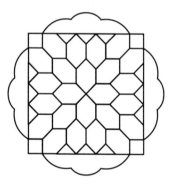

The seam is stitched right at the edge of the freezer paper. When all four scalloped borders are stitched onto the Hexagon block, press the seams toward the inside of the block.

Using a 3" square of Templar, press the seam allowance of the corners under, creating clean finished edges for appliqué. Use a small amount of starch painted on the seam allowances to set these corners.

Outer Green Border D

Curved pattern #3 on pages 132-135. From the length of the dark green fabric, cut four 84" strips 12" wide. Using the length rather than the width results in some added waste, but it yields a border without seams and less stretch. The top edge of each border needs to be marked for the serpentine curve that will be cut into it before being appliquéd onto the center and corner parts of the quilt.

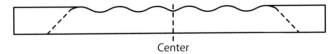

Center

For each side of the outer borders:
Mark the centerline.

Place the curved pattern aligned at the centerline and top edge. Trace the curve. Flip the pattern to reverse and mark the other half of the border. Cut the curves.

Note that the pattern includes the 45° miter. Be sure to mark this as well, but do not cut the miter. It is a guide. There should be a small bit of excess border on either end.

Aligning and Appliquéing the Border Pieces:

Center one of the border pieces onto the quilt. Pin generously to hold its position. It may be helpful to baste these border pieces rather than handling a quilt full of pins.

Align and pin the opposite side border onto the quilt. Then align the last two borders and pin on the quilt.

At this point, the four sides are pinned or basted into position: but where they join each other at the miters they are not.

Focusing on one corner at a time, leave one border piece entering the corner lying flat, while turning the other at the corner approximately 45° to create a miter. Use a 12" square rotary cutting guide with a 45° marked line to accurately check the miter placement. When good, pin this placement. It may be pressed, glue set, or basted to hold this position. Miter the remaining corners using the previous instruction.

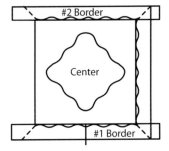

Appliqué the green outer border to the quilt either turning the edge under ¼" and hand appliquéing or using a machine technique. Hand stitch the miters.

From the backside, trim excess fabric from the miters leaving about ¼" – ⅜" and press the seams open. Trim the newly appliquéd seam of the outer border, removing all excess fabric from the body of the quilt. There should be ¼" – ⅜" at most in the seam.

The quilt is now ready for the ribbon and nosegay appliqués.

Ribbon Appliqué

The ribbon appliqué of the outer border is made up of seven unique pieces and their reverses. There are a total of 56 appliqué ribbon pieces to prep.

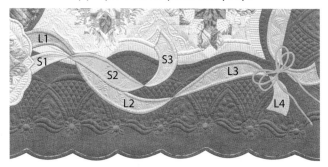

Use 4 shades of green silk, two shades of sage green (A, B), and two shades of kiwi green (C, D)

Coordinate your choices with the shades of green in your Hexagon blocks.

The change in color is very subtle, so the ribbons appear to flutter.

Pattern Piece	Color	Quantity
S1	C, D	Two of each color
S1 Reverse	C, D	Two of each color
S2	C, D	Two of each color
S2 Reverse	C, D	Two of each color
S3	C, D	Two of each color
S3 Reverse	C, D	Two of each color
L1	A, B	Two of each color
L1 Reverse	A, B	Two of each color
L2	A, B	Two of each color
L2 Reverse	A, B	Two of each color
L3	A, B	Two of each color
L3 Reverse	A, B	Two of each color
L4	A, B	Two of each color
L4 Reverse	A, B	Two of each color

Note: Color placement for the outer border appliqué ribbon is per the following schematic.

Color Placement for Ribbon Appliqué

A – Sage Green	C – Kiwi Green
B – Sage Green (little darker)	D – Kiwi Green (little darker)

Prepare each of the appliqué ribbon pieces for turned edge appliqué using one of the methods given, freezer paper or Templar. Note that pieces L1, L2, and S1 have one side which doesn't require turning under, as indicated on the pattern piece.

Position the ribbons on the quilt, confirming placement with the hexagon nosegays. Baste, pin, or glue into position and attach with the appliqué method of your choice, hand or machine.

Cut away any seam bulk from beneath the hexagon nosegays and the appliqué ribbons after they are securely appliquéd into position. Failure to do this will leave a lot of unnecessary bulk that will not lie properly when quilting.

Coral Shoestring Bows

Trace around the bow design and cut out a template from cardstock. Template on page 139.

One of the strings is longer than the other for a more natural look. I chose batik because it is tightly woven, doesn't ravel like regular cotton fabrics do, and appliqués beautifully.

Each bow requires approximately 42" of ⅜" bias strip. Seam the bias strip to get this length if needed, but clip the bias cut seam to ⅛" and be sure to press open. Also, try to place the seam where the bow's knot will be.

Note: The edges of this thin strip are needle-turned as the bow is appliquéd, rather than using the prepared edge technique shown througout this book. To stitch these bows down in one continuous pattern, follow the diagram for placement. Add the center knot appliqué last.

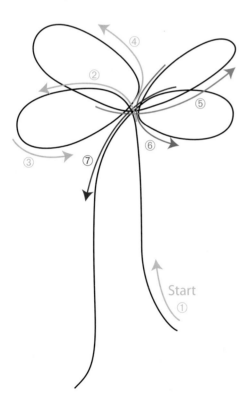

Appliqué Circles

Along the center medallion scalloped edge, using a variety of purple tones in both cotton and batik, make 24 turned edge ⅝" diameter circles. Appliqué just above the points of the scalloped edge.

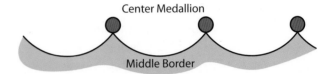

On the outer green border, uninterfaced silk Radiance in deep green that blends with the cotton fabric of the outer border, make 60 turned edge ⅝" diameter circles. Appliqué placement is shown in the following illustration, 15 per side.

On hexagon corners, make 24 circles ⅜" in diameter from champagne silk. Six circles are needed per corner.

Location for appliquéd ⅜" diameter silk circles

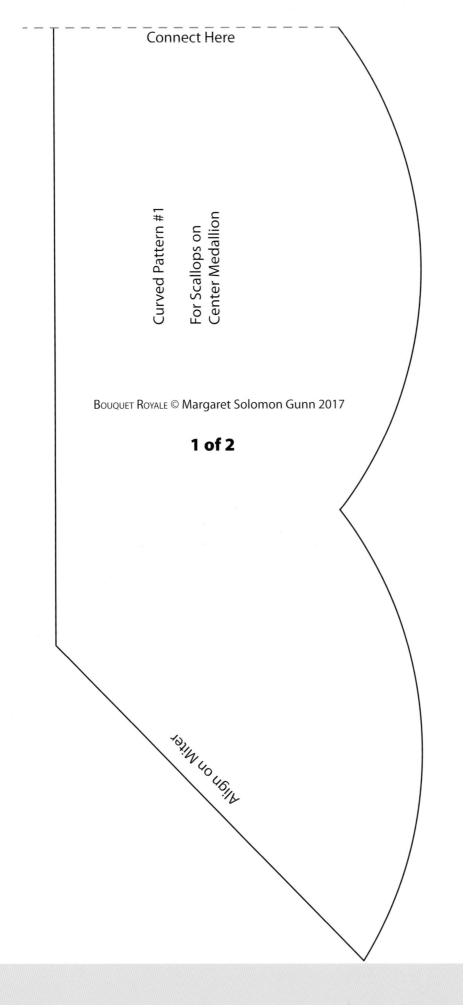

Connect Here

Curved Pattern #1

For Scallops on
Center Medallion

Bouquet Royale © Margaret Solomon Gunn 2017

1 of 2

Align on Miter

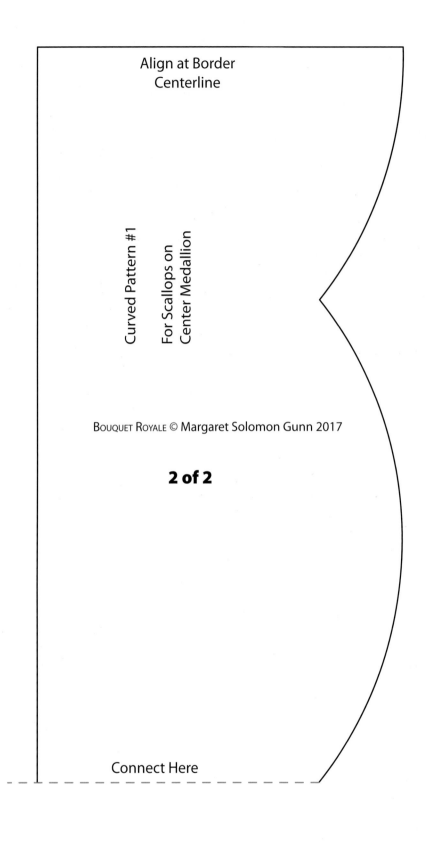

Align at Border
Centerline

Curved Pattern #1

For Scallops on
Center Medallion

BOUQUET ROYALE © Margaret Solomon Gunn 2017

2 of 2

Connect Here

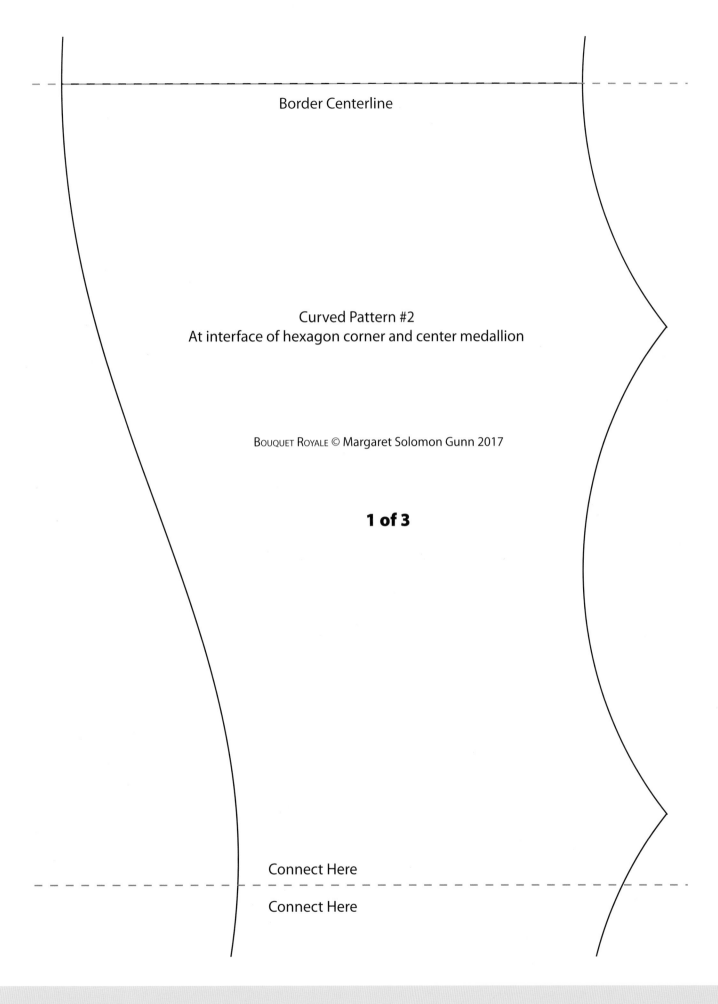

Border Centerline

Curved Pattern #2
At interface of hexagon corner and center medallion

BOUQUET ROYALE © Margaret Solomon Gunn 2017

1 of 3

Connect Here

Connect Here

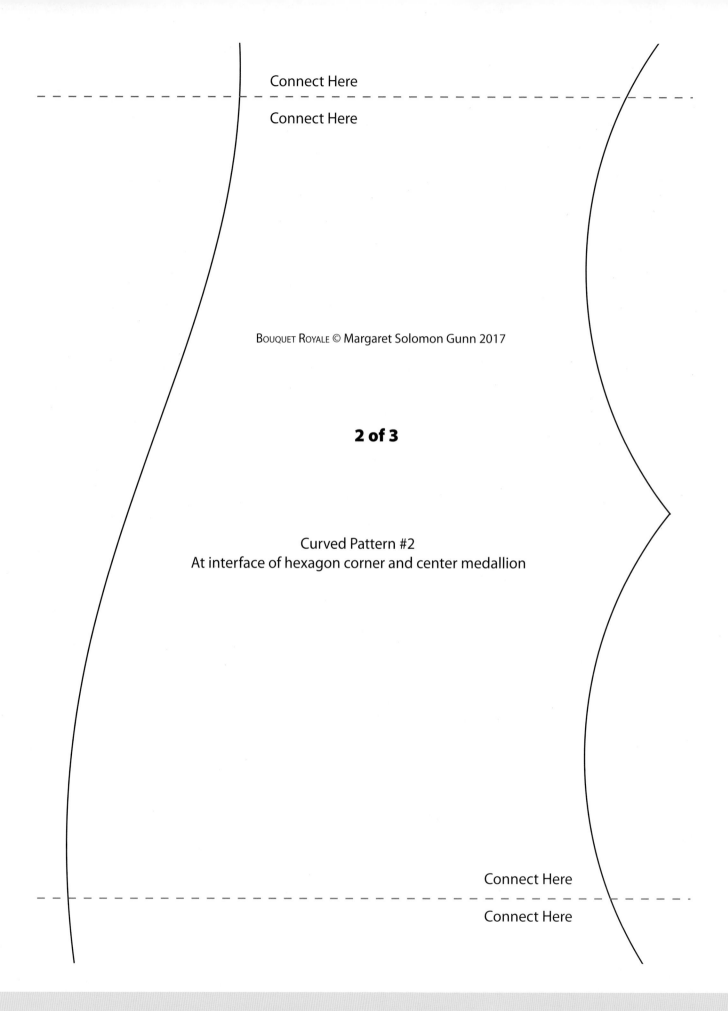

Connect Here

Connect Here

Bouquet Royale © Margaret Solomon Gunn 2017

2 of 3

Curved Pattern #2
At interface of hexagon corner and center medallion

Connect Here

Connect Here

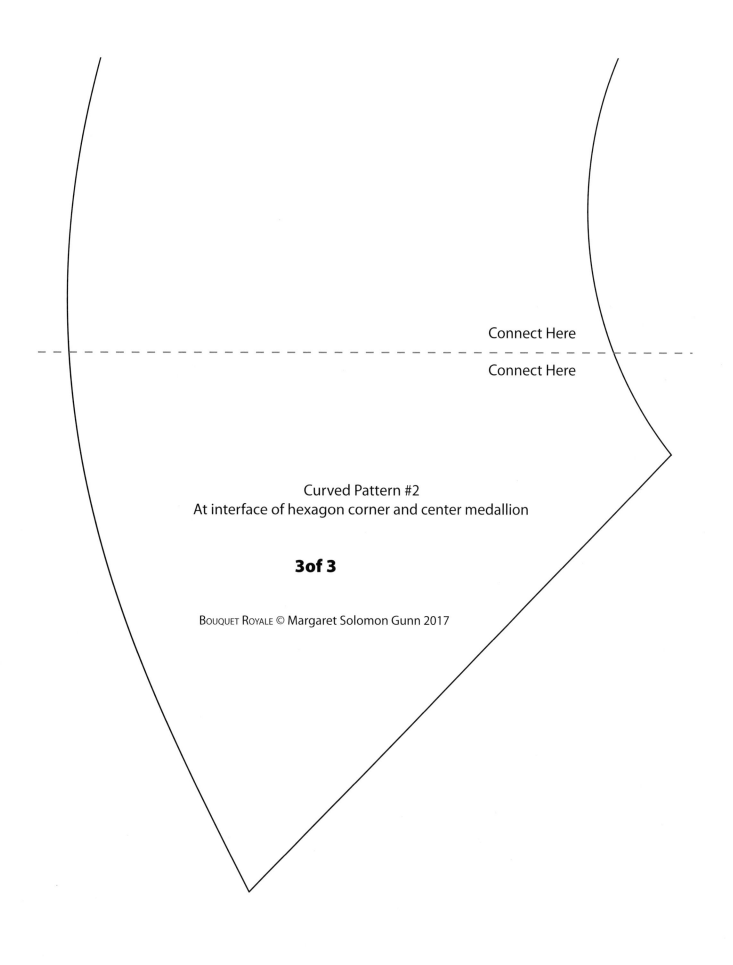

Connect Here

Connect Here

Curved Pattern #2
At interface of hexagon corner and center medallion

3of 3

BOUQUET ROYALE © Margaret Solomon Gunn 2017

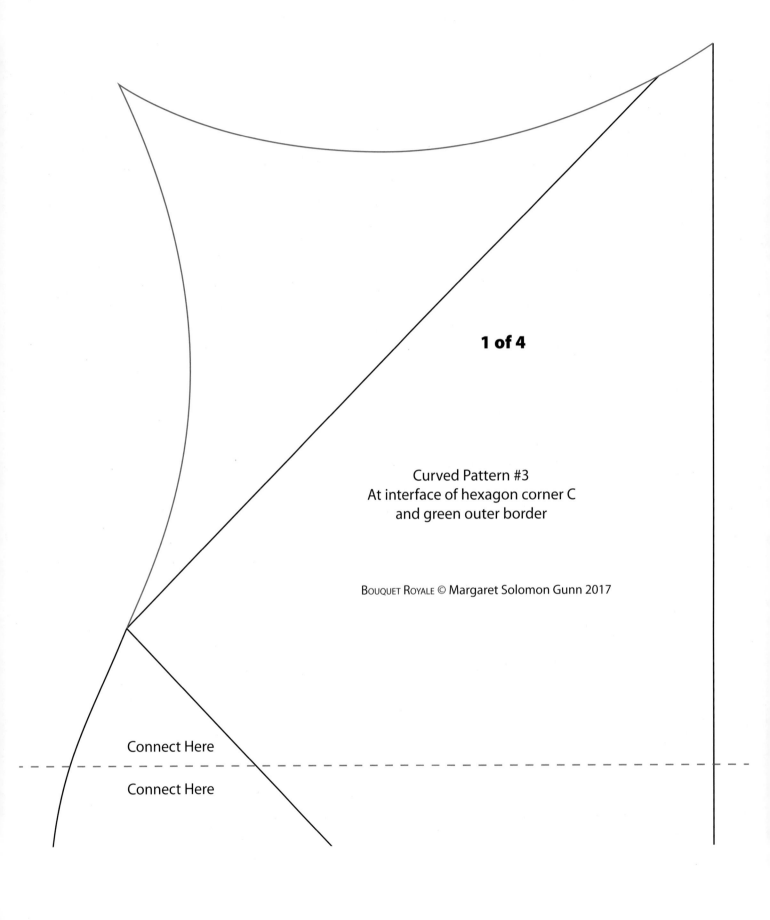

1 of 4

Curved Pattern #3
At interface of hexagon corner C
and green outer border

Bouquet Royale © Margaret Solomon Gunn 2017

Connect Here

Connect Here

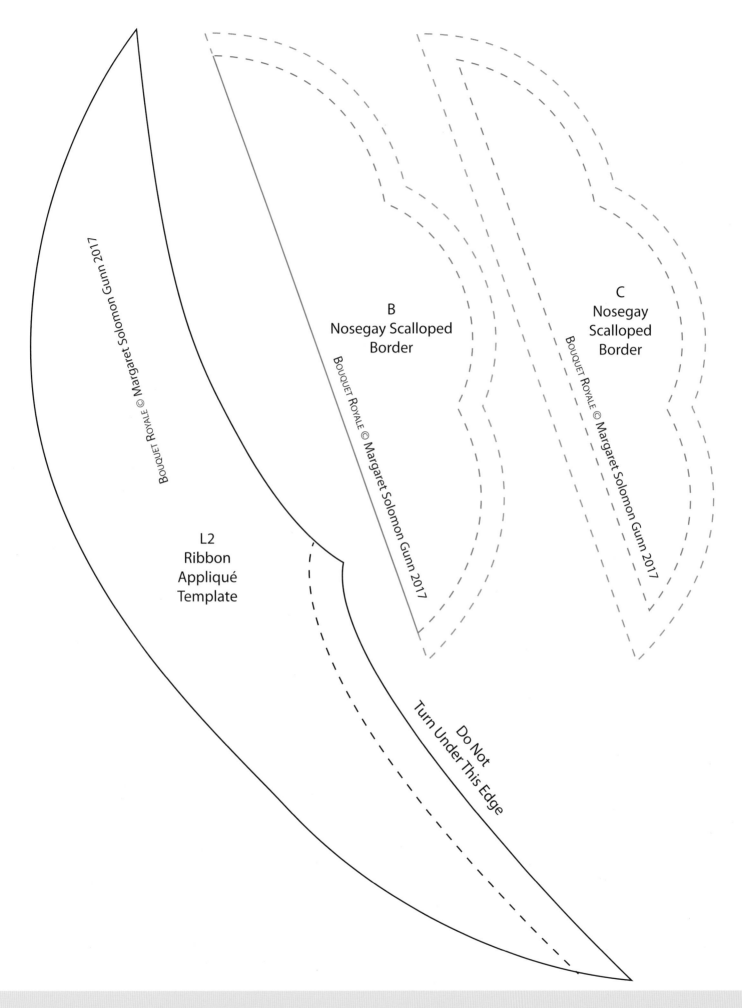

BOUQUET ROYALE © Margaret Solomon Gunn 2017

L2
Ribbon
Appliqué
Template

B
Nosegay Scalloped
Border

BOUQUET ROYALE © Margaret Solomon Gunn 2017

C
Nosegay
Scalloped
Border

BOUQUET ROYALE © Margaret Solomon Gunn 2017

Do Not
Turn Under This Edge

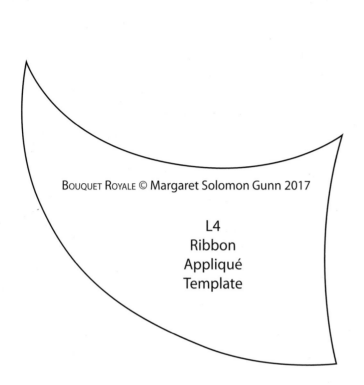

BOUQUET ROYALE © Margaret Solomon Gunn 2017

L4
Ribbon
Appliqué
Template

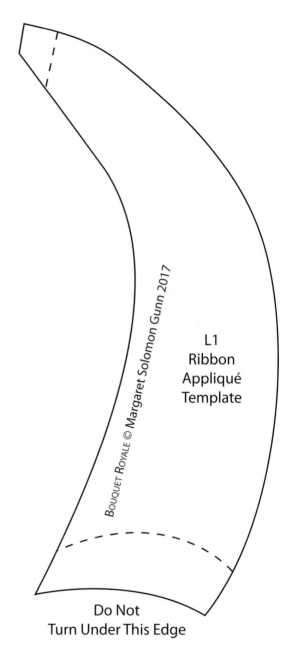

BOUQUET ROYALE © Margaret Solomon Gunn 2017

L1
Ribbon
Appliqué
Template

Do Not
Turn Under This Edge

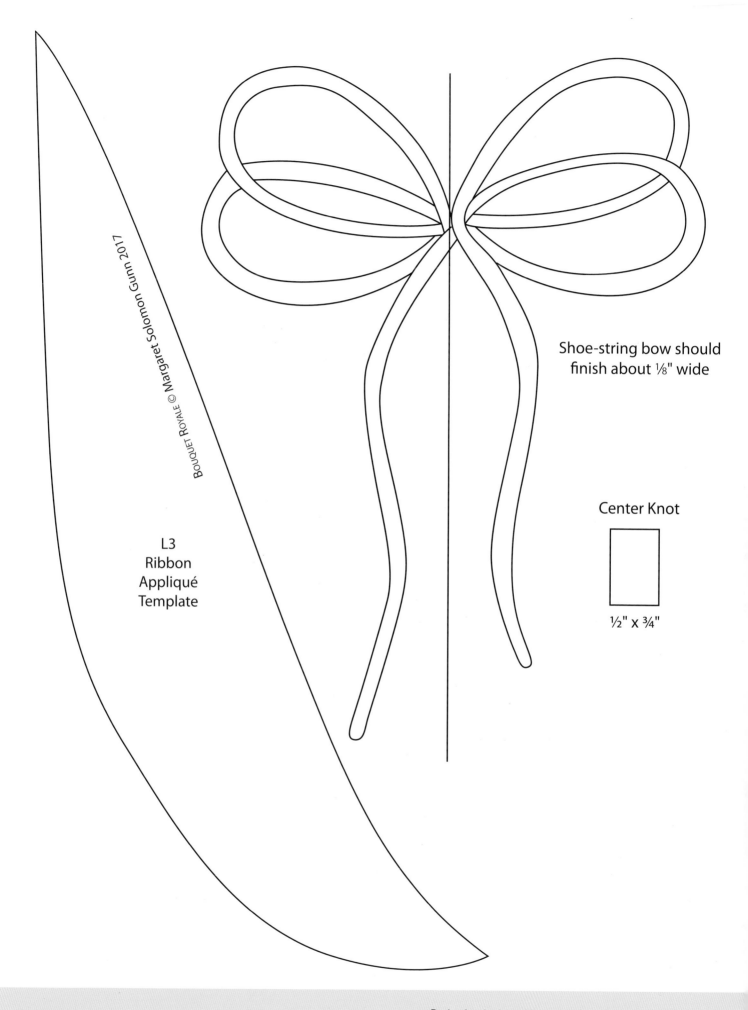

Bouquet Royale © Margaret Solomon Gunn 2017

L3
Ribbon
Appliqué
Template

Shoe-string bow should
finish about ⅛" wide

Center Knot

½" x ¾"

Quilting Motifs
BOUQUET ROYALE

BOUQUET ROYALE is an intricate quilt of colorful piecing and appliqué with no shortage of details. The quilting needed to reflect this, but at the same time unite and enhance the top. The goals of the quilting were to unify the 25 different Hexagon blocks, create a visual center for the quilt, and create quilting that follows the regal floral vibe of the quilt.

Required Tools:

• Air or water erasable marking pen and chalk marking pencil
• ¼" straight longarm template with ¼" etched lines
• 3", 4", 6", 8" diameter longarm circle or arc templates
• 12" diameter longarm curved crosshatch template
• Basketweave stencil by Emily Senuta or equivalent
• Variety of round longarm templates from 4" to 35" diameter (optional)
• Lightbox

Pieced Hexagon Blocks

While the Hexagon blocks are in many colors and fabrics, all are quilted similarly in an attempt to create unity on the quilt. Quilting each differently, perhaps following the different lines that the fussy cut piecing created, would only increase the chaos and busyness on the quilt. The only difference between the blocks was the color of thread that was chosen. I used a 40 wt. shiny thread because it would show above the prints—subtly, but it does show!

One of the things I strive toward when designing quilting is to create a pattern that is different from yet still complementary to the piecing. This design carries the floral theme of the quilt, while showing a nice variety of quilting motifs as well. Please note that the quilting of this block was designed to be attractive, while not necessarily expeditious to stitch. Those who prefer more continuous quilting may choose to modify the stitching.

The quilting is comprised of a central flower and leaves, crosshatching, a curved arc frame, and outer feathers.

Begin by stitching in the ditch around the outside of the printed hexagons. The location for the SID is shown as the outermost green line. Use a clear thread to be truly invisible.

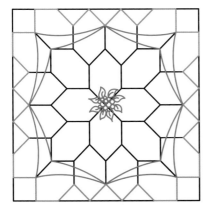

To quilt the frame, start your thread at the center point of any outer edge. Using the 12" curved template, quilt from this point to the corner as indicated above, quilting the frame that surrounds the block.

Upon reaching the starting point, align the template to quilt a curved line that ends at the inner point of the hexagon. When the starting point is reached, tie off and cut your thread. Nothing is marked. This is point-to-point quilting that uses the piecing to guide where to stitch.

For the flower and leaves, pull up your thread at the center of the block. A simple pattern of variably sized pebbles and a few flower petals is used to anchor the center of the block, giving the flower a floral appearance. At this point, the block is adequately stabilized and the remainder may be quilted without fear of distorting the lines of the piecing.

Stitch a petal-like shape in one of the four center hexagons. Follow the general shape of the piecing, but do not stitch in the ditch. This shape should have a softer, more organic appearance.

Now, create a similar type shape for the first leaf, following the general hexagon shape, but not the rigid lines of the piecing.

Continue the process described in the last two steps, going around the inner part of the block alternately quilting the petals and leaves.

When you reach the starting point, add one last row of echo stitching to all four petals. This line of quilting is approximately ⅛" inboard from the first stitching. The reason I stitch the second outline is because it helps to emphasize its shape, making it a little puffier. Quilting, after all, is about creating designs that show, and this can often be a challenge with busy prints. Tie off, clip, and bury your threads.

The ¼" curved crosshatching can be stitched separately in four sections, or continuously. Let's first look at the mechanics of curved crosshatching and you can decide if you want to quilt them continuously or not.

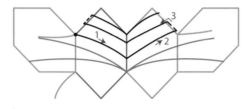

Prepare to quilt at the location indicated above. This is ¼" from the quilted frame. The lines that will be quilted are indicated in black on this illustration. Placing the 12" arc template right at the edge of the frame, stitch to the seam at the block centerline following line 1. With your needle down, stop and reposition the template to stitch ¼" from the next frame, ending at the hexagon seam in line 2. Backtrack along the hexagon seam ¼" shown at line 3, reposition the template and stitch another curved line that is ¼" from the first one. Repeat this process until all lines in one direction are stitched.

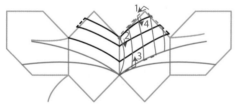

Carefully back track along the inner boundary of the crosshatching to get to the center at the pink dot shown above where the crosshatch lines for the opposite direction begin. Quilt ¼" spaced crosshatching on one side of the center following lines 2, 3, and 4. Then backtrack to the starting pink dot to stitch the lines on the other side.

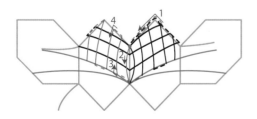

At this point, you can tie off and stitch the next section of crosshatching or backtrack around the perimeter of the flower and leaf to get to where the next section of crosshatching starts. A fine quilting thread will not show significantly if you backtrack, but this is a choice that you will have to make.

The feathers, shown in green, are stitched using the outer edge of the frame as their spine. They are quilted in eight separate sections. I chose to carefully quilt formal (aka bump back) feathers, but really any type of feather would be lovely here. Be creative!

Outer Border

The quilting of the 10" wide outer green border is comprised of several different components, each of which was selected to create texture, movement of the eye, and cohesion with other areas of the quilt. Let's step through how each section is marked and some of the rationale for why it was designed the way it was. The quilting was designed to lie behind the silk appliquéd ribbons, sort of a peek-a-boo design. As a result, some of the necessary markings described will actually involve marking of the appliqué ribbons rather than the green outer border fabric.

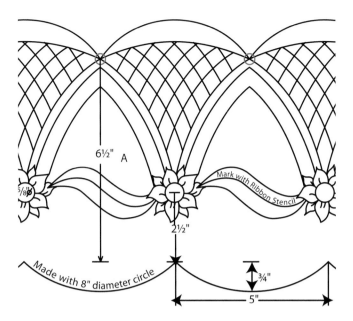

6½" A

Mark with Ribbon Stencil

⅝"

2½"

Made with 8" diameter circle

¾"

5"

Prior to quilting, I recommend marking the outer scalloped edge. Doing this allows you to tailor your quilting to this edge. Also mark the apex of the cathedral window as indicated with red circles before quilting, ideally while the quilt is on a table. It is easier to get accurate measurements when the quilt is lying flat, rather than while it is loaded on a longarm frame. All other quilting is done freehand using the guidelines on the templates and the silk dot centers of the border's flowers.

The flowers are each stitched individually. You can use one design or a combination of a couple different flowers. Bouquet Royale has two flower designs. Make patterns or templates by sizing the illustration to yield a ⅝" diameter center circle.

The flowers are quilted with a 40 wt. GLIDE thread in a slightly contrasting color so the stitching stands out

more. While I try to design quilting to be as continuous as possible, since stops and starts are extremely time consuming, I wanted only the flower design to stand out in the contrasting thread. As a result, the flowers must be quilted one at a time. The remainder of the quilting on the border is stitched with a 100 wt. coordinating green silk thread. This particular thread is very thin and backtracking one or even two times is nearly unnoticeable. It is much easier to stitch several areas without tying off the thread.

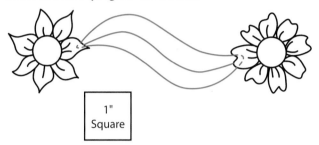

1"
Square

Make a template of the ribbon stencil shown above in red, taking care to enlarge until the reference square measures exactly 1" square. While cardstock works relatively well, a clear template plastic may be better as its transparency yields better visibility for aligning. Using a chalk marking pencil, mark the location of the quilted ribbons. Each ribbon flows between the centers of adjacent flowers. The line down the center of the ribbon may be freehand quilted.

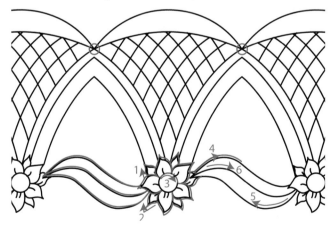

Restart at the flower on the far left with a silk thread. Stitch a tight echo around the flower shown as lines 1 and 2 in the above illustration. The echo should be barely ¹⁄₁₆" outside of the lines of the flower. This outlining will help to pop the flower enhancing its visibility. Now, stitch through the flower and around the flower's center (3) to get to the other side where the next ribbon starts. Stitch the ribbon freehand following the marked upper and lower lines 4 and 5, and then quilt a line down the center of the ribbon following line 6. It is possible to quilt continuously down the row of flowers echoing a flower, then quilting a ribbon, then echoing the next flower until all flowers and ribbons are quilted.

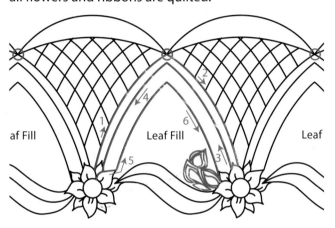

Next, the frames of the cathedral windows are stitched. The stitching path for these is indicated with green numbered arrows on the above illustration. These require a 12" circular arc with etched concentric curved lines. I use the Boomerang template made by Deloa Jones, but this industry has several options. Begin by aligning the template with the visual center of the flower center at one end with the marked red apex circle at the other end. Begin stitching where the arc intersects the flower's echo quilting at the dot at the beginning of line 1. Stitch up to the apex of the arch following line 1. With the needle in down position, reposition the template to now align to the center of the next flower. Stitch to where the arc intersects the echo quilting along line 2. Next, stitch an echo line ¼" beneath the first arch to create a frame following lines 3 and 4. Use the echo stitching around the flower to carefully travel to the next stitching location.

Place a second frame on the cathedral window, this time ½" below the first frame following lines 5 and 6. Use of double frames makes the arches appear more prominent.

The area beneath the outlined frames is quilted with a leaf filler. This fill creates organic, leaf like shapes approximately ¾" – 1" tall and about ³⁄₈" – ½" wide. Making them smaller than this will limit the amount of visible texture. Echo stitching one or two times ¹⁄₁₆" outside the initial leaf reinforces the shape. Be sure to randomize the direction that they point. To keep the stitching as continuous as possible, try to stitch the leaf fill in a circular sweep so you end close to where you started. Carefully retrace over any stitching and across the top petals of the flower to get to the starting point for the next cathedral arch.

Cathedral arches are topped with scallops and the subsequent triangular arched shape is curve crosshatched. Placing the more rigid, geometric quilting beside the free form leafy filler creates a visually appealing juxtaposition. The difference of the two styles of quilting, as well as the double framing on the cathedral window help both quilting designs to show more than if they were used individually.

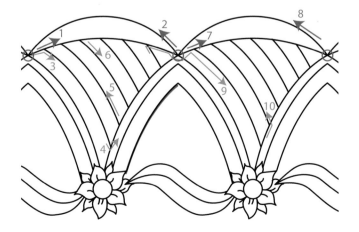

Quilting in a continuous fashion, begin at the red circle at the top of a cathedral window arch. Using a 12" diameter circle or 12" arc, connect the tops of two adjacent cathedral windows by stitching the lower scallop along line 1. With a smaller 8" diameter circle, return to the starting point along line 2. The 12" diameter curved crosshatch ruler is used to stitch the ½" spaced curved lines. My method stitches all the lines in one direction first following lines 3-6, then the quilting proceeds to the next scallop following lines 7 and 8, and finally the section of crosshatch lines following lines 9 and 10.

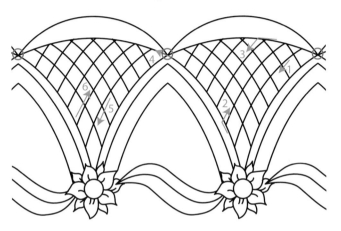

When you reach the last section of crosshatching, reverse direction and stitch the curved crosshatching of the other direction, travelling from right to left filling each section continuously.

The outermost area of the quilt between the flowers, ribbons, and the scalloped edge is stitched with very narrow parallel lines. The lines are typically less than ⅛" apart. I used a ruler to keep the lines straight, but the actual spacing was more or less eye balled. This very tight, linear quilting does two things. It creates an intensely textural edge to the quilt. It also is the catalyst to pop the flowers and ribbons to the positive making them more visible. This could be done with almost any tight filler, even stippling, but the linear edge makes a more refined look.

A row of ⅜" diameter pebbles are freehand quilted at the serpentine boundary between the champagne silk and the green outer border. Refer to the quilting of AUTUMN'S SURRENDER for possible stitching techniques for pebbles. Placing a more curved motif, like the pebbles, beside the linear, parallel lines of the silk makes both motifs show that much more.

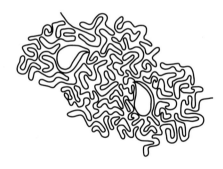

Outboard of the pebbles and above the arches, a stylized stippling is quilted. It is tight, so that the areas of positive relief such as the scalloped arches really show. There are also randomly placed teardrops within the stipple simply for visual interest, as stippling can get visually boring by itself.

Hexagon Corner Setting Square and Triangles

The quilting design for the silk Radiance squares and the setting triangles of the four hexagon corners consists of a floral feathery outer frame, a scalloped

¼" middle frame, and a medallion center which is filled with a basket weave design.

Scale the design to 6" for the indicated distance. Mark the design onto the appropriate squares and triangles of the quilt using a lightbox, taking care to center the pattern in the square. The pattern will be stitched on point. Because these areas of BOUQUET ROYALE are light colored fabric, I marked using a water soluble blue pen.

The design is stitched in two threads, a 40 wt. GLIDE (color: Prickly Pear) for the frames and some fills, and a cream 100 wt. silk for areas of background filler around the floral feathery frame, stipples, and outside linear fill.

The curved arcs of the medallion center are stitched using an 8" diameter circle template. It is filled with a basket weave pattern created from an Emily Senuta stencil. The design is backfilled to bring a dense pop of the golden thread color to the block, making the pattern and its frame more visible. Using stencils to accent quilting designs is a fantastic option, especially for those that do not have computerized machines and the library of digital designs available. Stencils come in

a multitude of patterns and sizes and can help take the guesswork out of what to stitch.

The basket weave pattern looks challenging, but it is simple to quilt and stitches up continuously. Start by quilting around the four sides of a tiny square, then densely stipple or fill the space, exiting at the opposite corner.

Traverse the short distance to the next small square space and do the same procedure. Follow the pattern and fill the squares continuously in a row, then move to the next row and do the same technique. Be sure to use a short stitch length so that the fill appears smooth.

The scallops of the middle frame are quilted using a 6" diameter circle. Between the center medallion and middle border, the area is quilted with pebbles. The pebble filler creates texture and color. Smaller pebbles create more color and will pop the frame more.

The floral feather frame is also stitched with the colored GLIDE thread. Unfortunately, it is not a continuous design and requires four starts and stops to quilt.

At this point, load a fine silk thread for the denser fills. The area between the middle frame and the floral feather frame is filled with a dense stipple. Dense quilting makes the details of the border more evident.

Outboard of the floral feathery frame I stitched a linear pattern consisting of ⅛" spaced lines in a boxlike layout. It was challenging, and I likely would not select this particular fill for this space again because of the immense time it required. As an easier and better alternative, consider quilting ⅛" lines perpendicularly placed to the edge of the floral feathery frame shown on the previous page.

Ribbon Appliqué

The appliqué ribbons on BOUQUET ROYALE are too large to leave unquilted. They appear floppy, as shown above. The loft that shows in the photo will decrease with time because the batting beneath the ribbon appliqué will shift around.

All of the on-appliqué quilting can be stitched continuously, but before stitching anything on the appliqués, they should be ditch stitched. All stitching

on the appliqués is done with a silk 100 wt. thread, as it blends beautifully on the silk and does not become thready on densely stitched fills.

A modified onion peel filler was chosen for the ribbons, as this appears to oscillate as a waving ribbon might. Before stitching this filler, a frame was quilted around the border of each piece of ribbon appliqué. The frame is about ⅜" from the edge and gives the ribbon added definition.

To further separate this frame from the filler, a second line of framing is stitched. This line is placed a scant ⅛" from the first line of stitching. Both of these lines of quilted framing are quilted using a variety of curved templates. Basically, I use whichever circle or arc is closest to the desired arc I want to stitch, choosing from templates ranging in size from 4" - 35" in diameter. This is a time when being a template junkie is helpful!

Next, mark a gentle and undulating line down the middle of the appliqué ribbon using chalk or your favorite marking pen. This gives you a guide of where the onion peel filler will change direction.

Starting on one side, stitch a gentle S shape back and forth until reaching the marked line. These lines should be fairly close together, about ⅛" to create quilting that is solely in the negative space.

Now, switch and make the S lines in the next marked area heading the opposite direction. Repeat this procedure until the onion peel filler is completed.

If there is another section of ribbon appliqué at the end of the one just quilted, simply stitch to the tip of it and begin the same sequence of steps. Make the process as continuous as possible.

Nosegays

The four appliquéd nosegays are each simply a pieced Hexagon block with a scalloped silk appliqué border. The quilting on these consists of a ¼" echo to enhance the scalloping shape of the nosegay, a circle of feathers, and basic rays that emanate from the block, all stitched in the 40 wt. thread. It is an uncomplicated, graceful, and sophisticated look.

The sequence of quilting for the appliquéd nosegays: Begin by outline stitching around the perimeter of the appliqué with clear thread shown in the illustration in pink. The Hexagon block would already be SID as a part of quilting the block.

A ¼" echo is placed just inside of the block boundary shown here in green. The curves are stitched with 3" and 4" circle templates. This line of echo quilting emphasizes the shape of the design.

With a 12" circle or arc template, quilt the two arcs indicated in gold spaced ⅛" apart. The outer arc serves as the spine for the feathers.

Lastly, the rays are stitched, shown here in blue. These may be quilted continuously if you are careful backtracking over tracing existing quilting lines.

Center Medallion

The quilting of the center medallion is comprised of several components: a floral motif, feathered scallop detail, faux nosegay quilting, and the central motif. Let's discuss each.

The center medallion has a floral motif located in four places along the outer border. It is quilted using colored thread and should measure 6" from end to end. One of the best ways to create a cohesive quilting plan for an entire quilt is to repeat designs or parts of designs on other areas of the quilt. A larger, more detailed version of this design was previously presented and used for the blank squares of the hexagon corners.

The outer scalloped border of the center medallion is framed with freehand quilted feathers. These are somewhat organic in that leaves are added to the design. The long, curving tendril is used as the spine and allows the feathers to switch direction. Quilting is all about creating movement and that is exactly what this does.

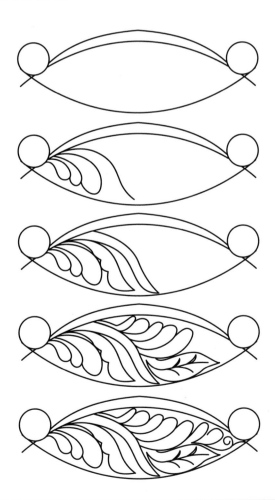

The five steps to create this design are simple. The first step is always to outline stitch the boundary of the silk and the green, then to quilt the other arches between the purple dots. This is accomplished with an 8" diameter arc or circle template. Note that the entire row may be quilted continuously, one scallop after another. Upon completing this, restart and quilt the feather motif, filling all scallops one after another as well. After quilting the leaf, trace along its inboard side and fill the remaining area of the scallop with a couple more feathers, finishing with a curlicue. This should position you conveniently to sneak to the next scallop for feathering.

The quilting design from the four appliquéd nosegays is utilized in the center medallion of the quilt too, creating faux nosegays from quilting. The scalloped frame motif is repeated in five places on the center medallion, four corners, and the center. This repetition brings cohesion, as well as the essence of the floral garden to this area. The scalloped border frame may be marked prior to loading or during the quilting.

Make a Nosegay Scallop template from the illustration on the next page, taking care that it is sized appropriately. After the scalloped frame is marked, the interior quilting of the four corner blocks is identical to what was just discussed for the appliquéd nosegays.

The block at the center of the quilt is treated a little differently. While the scalloped edge frame of the nosegays is also copied here, the general appearance is intentionally grander. It is important for quilts to have a visual center. This is a natural point that will grab the viewer's eye. Sometimes this visual center is created with the piecing and appliqué, other times, when the piecing is nearly identical, it needs to be created with quilting. It is interesting to mention that this visual center is not always at the center of the quilt. For BOUQUET ROYALE, however, it is at the center. An attempt has been made, therefore, to make the center quilting more prominent since there is no piecing to do that job. Motifs like the fans, the feathers, and dense stippling were chosen to set this area apart.

Begin with the fans quilted at the four corners of the center block. Using a 12" arc, stitch the outer frame indicated here in blue. It is just point-to-point quilting. Next, start at the pink dot located at the base of the fan and quilt a line of echo quilting ¼" inward from the first frame shown here in pink. Upon reaching the starting point, using the same arc template, stitch fanned lines outward shown in green. I divided this space into five spaces, but any equal spacing will look good. With all four fans quilted, you are now ready to quilt the scallops and feathers around the center block.

Mark the nosegay scallops with the Nosegay Scallop template and then stitch. Echo quilt these curves twice to give increased prominence using 3" and 4" circle templates as before. Interior feathers are omitted and the space is densely stippled to show the distinct difference in thread color. Larger feathers are quilted on the outside of the scalloped frame instead. My intent with this center block was to make the quilting blend cohesively with the other nosegay blocks, while also making it stand out with visual difference as well.

Scallop Quilting Template

BOUQUET ROYALE © Margaret Solomon Gunn 2017

Preparing Turned Edge Appliqué

The appliqué for the quilts in this book are all turned edge using one of two techniques, Templar or freezer paper. The following tutorials show steps for preparing appliqué. Two are specific to any shape appliqué patch, while one is specific to circles. Try each technique and determine which works best for you.

Appliqué with Templar Templates

Templar is high temperature plastic, which tolerates the heat of an iron without melting or significantly deforming. Templar is clear, so visibility is better than working with freezer paper. Templar is available in sheets that can be cut to any appliqué shape.

When cutting out the Templar pattern with scissors, all edges must be smooth as any bumps on the template will be transferred to the actual appliqué patch. Smooth the edges of the Templar template with a piece of 800 grit sandpaper or a smooth nail file.

Indicate the right side of the template with a designation like right or top. Because these templates are identical from either side, it is easy to mix up the directionality and get them reversed.

Templar templates can be reused dozens of times. Once they start to deform slightly, make another template. This is an advantage over the freezer-paper method when numerous identical patches need to be prepared. Additionally, the appliqué patches can be prepared days or weeks in advance, as long as they are stored flat in a container.

Starch and sizing do similar things. Starch is a vegetable based product used in the garment cleaning business to stiffen fabrics. Sizing, a synthetic product, is used to add body and crispness to whatever is pressed. It tends to be lighter weight than most starches. Sizing does not tend to leave a white, flaky residue that some starches can leave. That said, light use of starch leaves very little residue.

My local stores do not always stock sizing, so I use a starch on my fabrics. Soaking quilts during the blocking process removes any finishing products, with flakiness or not, from the fabric. This technique works well with either starch or sizing, so each quilter can decide which is best for them.

Prepare by spraying the starch into a cup, allow the bubbles to disappear, and paint the edge of the fabric and the seam allowance with a nylon paint brush.

Materials:

Templar
Pencil
Spray starch or sizing liquefied in a cup
Nylon paintbrush
Iron

General Instructions

Trace the outline of the appliqué patch onto Templar and cut out the template on the line with paper or non-sewing scissors.

Place the Templar template right side down on the reverse side of the fabric and trace the Templar template.

Looking at the backside of the fabric, you do not want to see the word *right* on the template, as this is not the right side of the fabric. Use pencil rather than an air or water erasable pen, because if the pen has not disappeared, it is more likely to be heat set with the iron. You also need a small cup of liquefied spray starch or sizing and a nylon paint brush.

Cut out the shape drawn on fabric leaving ³⁄₁₆" outside the pencil marking. The lower edge of this piece will go into a ¼" seam so leave a ¼" seam allowance.

Paint the liquefied starch or sizing onto the seam allowance outside the pencil markings.

It is important to recognize if this patch needs clipping for the seam allowances to lie smoothly. An example of an appliqué patch taken from the ZEN GARDEN quilt is shown here. The key beneath the illustration denotes if clipping is needed to make curves lie properly.

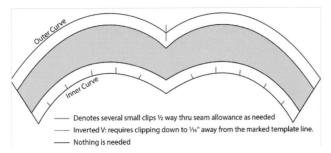

Note that these clipping guidelines also apply for the Templar method or the freezer paper method. This example shape includes an outer curve along the top of the patch, an inner curve along the bottom of the patch, and an inside point.

Let's look at how these three examples in the above illustration need to be handled prior to turning the edge.

The outer curve is fine as it is. No clipping is necessary. The inner curves will only lie smoothly if they are clipped. As shown on the figure, make clips every half inch or so. These clips should only pass through about half of the seam allowance or ⅛" deep.

The inverted V or inside point at the top of the patch must receive a perpendicular snip inwards to about 3-4 threads or ¹⁄₁₆" of the actual template. This is a deeper snip than inner curves require.

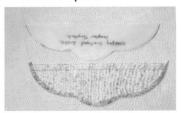

Work your way around the appliqué patch with the iron, pressing the seam allowance onto the Templar beginning at the inverted V locations. Hold the iron 20-30 seconds until the starch dries.

Take care not to create any creases in the curve. If a crease results, rewet with starch and repeat the procedure. A crease that shows on the front side is not desirable.

When all the edges are turned under, let the patch cool a few seconds and remove the Templar template.

The patch is now ready to be hand or machine stitched to the quilt.

Freezer Paper Turned Edge Appliqué

Freezer paper can be purchased at most grocery stores. Oddly, I have found that it is not a product that I can predictably find at a grocery, but a local meat market always carries it.

Often, a single thickness of freezer paper makes a decent appliqué template for most cotton fabrics. When working with the interfaced silk Radiance, two thicknesses of freezer paper pressed together yields a better edge.

Tools Needed:

Freezer paper
Glue stick
Pencil
Scissors

General Instructions

Because the freezer paper will be ironed onto the reverse side of the fabric, the pattern for the patch needs to be reversed before tracing it onto the freezer paper unless it is symmetrical.

Place the freezer paper over the reversed pattern of the appliqué patch. If it is not possible to see the boundary of the pattern, either hold it up against a window or use a lightbox. Trace the applique shape onto the non-shiny side of the freezer paper.

If a second sheet of freezer paper is needed, cut one out, press the two sheets together, and cut out the template.

Press the freezer paper to the backside of the fabric using a dry iron.

Trim the fabric about ³⁄₁₆" to ¼" outside of the freezer paper. This piece will need a ¼" seam allowance at the bottom since it is stitched into a regular seam.

Identify any areas that need to be clipped and clip them.

There are many glue sticks commercially available. Some quilters prefer ones that can be purchased at quilt shops, as they have a smaller surface area. Other quilters use a clear liquid glue dispensed through a micro-nozzle. Personally, I have tried a number of different brands of glue sticks and the Elmer's glue sticks work as well as most others at a much lower cost. Since I always soak my quilts as a part of blocking them once the quilting is completed, I don't worry about leaving glue stick in my quilts. If using glue on your quilt bothers you, then the Templar method may be a better choice.

Gently place a light covering of glue on the outer ¼" of the freezer paper. It does not need to be glopped on thick and heavy. Its only purpose is to hold the turned edge snugly to the template until it is appliquéd in place.

Finger press the seam onto the freezer paper making sure there are no creases at the curved edge.

Stitch the appliqué patch into its position on the quilt, either using tiny hand stitches or whatever machine technique you prefer.

For hand stitching, consider using a 60-100 wt. fine thread in a color matching the appliqué patch. Threads

I like include Superior Kimono silk, Superior Bottom Line and WonderFil's InvisaFil, as all are essentially invisible when stitched.

Once the patch is appliquéd into position, dampen the perimeter of the patch where the turned edge and glue is located using water and a small paint brush. This will release the glue. If it does not, there will be better access to the glued area after the backside is snipped open.

Next, make a snip on the backside of the backing fabric, leaving an access hole to the back of the appliqué patch. Small pointy embroidery scissors work well for this task. Depending on the size of the patch, the freezer paper can be removed with your fingers. Smaller patches may be more easily removed with long tweezers.

Note: From my years of longarm quilting, I glean that many quilters are uncomfortable cutting the backing behind their appliqués. Some quilters leave layer upon layer of appliqués, as well as any seam bulk that may have resulted from piecing. I am a firm believer that this must be cut away to yield a nice and flat looking appliqué patch. Fear not, your quilting will hold everything in place, forever.

Preparing Turned Edge Circles
The edges of circle appliqué patches can be prepared using the following tutorial. This tutorial uses Karen Kay Buckley's Perfect Circles™ or a circle cut from Templar of a desired diameter.

Tools Needed:
Karen Kay Buckley's Perfect Circles or Templar circle
Needle/thread
Spray starch or sizing liquefied in a cup
Nylon paintbrush
Iron
Scissors

Cut a fabric circle about ⅜"-½" larger in diameter than the desired finished circle size.

With hand needle and thread, make a row of running stitches ⅛" from the outer edge of the circles, knotting one end. I use a typical thread that would be used for piecing, 40-50 wt. cotton.

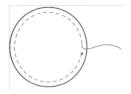 

Lay the circle template in the center of the stitched fabric circle.

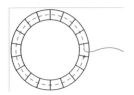 

Cinch the fabric tight around the circle template. Smooth the fabric around the circle template with your fingernail.

Paint starch on the part that wraps the template with liquid starch or sizing.

Wrap the tail of the thread around the circle a few times to temporarily secure and place an iron on the circle.

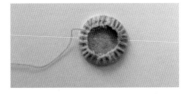

When the starch is dry, remove the iron, allow the circle to cool, and remove the template.

These prepared appliqué patches and prepared circles can be made up and stored for weeks until you are ready to stitch them onto the quilt.

A Few Words from Margaret

Lessons learned in my quilting journey:

~ Trust your own instincts. If somebody tells you your fabric choice is not right for the piece you are making, but you still love it, who cares. It is yours.

~ Use colors that make you want to do cartwheels, not the fads that everyone else may be flocking toward.

~ Work toward your own timetable. Some may make a quilt in a weekend, but it is ok if it takes 18 months too.

~ Your quilt; your rules.

~Take time to play. If you are always "working" on a project, it can feel like work. Taking downtime to do something different often recharges your batteries.

~I have accrued at least a dozen good cover-up techniques for when things don't go just right. Don't consider these ways to hide mistakes, but rather design alterations!

~ This list could go on for days. You don't quilt 6+ hours a day for 7 years and not accumulate an ongoing list of pertinent lessons. Without doubt, I have accrued a long list of quilting how-to's, but the personal things learned are equally as important.

Never forget that this is an individual journey. You may have friends that are working in the same business, but your success is based on your scale of success, not someone else's. One person will be happy with one level of success, whereas another just happens to define it at a higher or lower level. Neither is right, just different.

What has pushed me further in the business is that I am the one that will pick out stitches at the sight of a small tension anomaly, when another might not be bothered quite as much. I may be more detail oriented than others, but that is me. It does not have to be you. Ultimately, you define your rules and benchmarks. Be happy where you are at a given time. This is an amazing journey, one that I liken occasionally to the Cinderella story. There is no point in going down this journey if you are not fully loving it. Today's bump in the road will be tomorrow's "aha moment."

ENJOY THESE AND MORE FROM AQS

AQS Publishing brings the latest in quilt topics to satisfy the traditional to modern quilter. Interesting techniques, vivid color, and clear directions make these books your one-stop for quilt design and instruction. With its leading Quilt-Fiction series, mystery, relationship, and community all merge as stories are pieced together to keep you spell-bound.

#12534 $24.95	#12526 $19.95	#12528 $24.95
#12520 $24.95	#12532 $24.95	#10274 $24.95
#12510 $24.95	#12524 $22.95	#12512 $21.95

AQS publications are available nationwide. Call or visit AQS
www.shopAQS.com
1-800-626-5420